For the Mighty BF
(BOOTS)

DAWN FRENCH

ME • YOU
A DIARY

Loads of help from Abi Thomas
Illustrations by Chris Burke

MICHAEL JOSEPH
an imprint of
PENGUIN BOOKS

Hello

Welcome to our diary.

This is a guilt-free zone.

You cannot get it wrong.

Use and abuse this book any way you want.
Write your appointments in it, birthdays to
remember, lists, key dates, thoughts, feelings and
reminders of... say. who to kill and when, and in
what order....

It's a way for us to spend a year together, to
celebrate the patterns and changes in the year,
along with the twists and turns, the surprises,
the hurts and the delights.

Every now and then, I've made places for you to
join me in some silliness or some thinking. Plus,
I've written some of my own thoughts about the
seasons and the months and other stuff, to
see us through.

By the end of the year, I am hoping you
will have a fatter, scruffier book that is
totally personalized by you.

I hope it becomes a treasure of your
making. Over to you.

Come on in, the paper is lovely....

You

Please place a current photo of yourself here.
It's best if it's a head-and-shoulders shot,
but anything will do.

1. Age: ....

2. Full name: ....

3. Photo was taken (when?): ....

4. Photo was taken (where?): ....

5. State of mind when photo was taken: ....

....

6. Best thing about that day: ....

....

7. Thing I like most in this photo: ....

....

....

8. Thing I like least in this photo: ....

....

....

9. Three words to describe who I see in this photo: ....

....

....

....

....

JANUARY

Look, the fact is we all have to START SOMEWHERE. Don't know about you, but I'm a bit tired after the clamour and busy-ness of Christmas, but in a couple of minutes I won't be, I'll be ready to wake up the year and get going. I know the dark mornings don't help. Why do they feel so ungodly? Is it that we feel like we're getting up in the middle of the night when we should still be curled up? I try to combat those odd sluggish, grumpy sensations by imagining I am stealing some extra night time to add to my day, a bit like I used to as a very young person when a night of fun ended with a slightly wobbly walk home in the gloamy low light of just before sunrise. Alongside the confidence of residual tipsiness was the thrill of being sexily nocturnal. Part cat, part lush, part party. Sort of Italian or French or whoever it is that staggers home in heels and a well-cut mac with make-up in interesting disarray. Moody, complicated, enigmatic and continental. Recently sexed, and slightly slovenly.

Nothing was further from the truth of course. I would more likely be in Doc Martens and denim overalls, with badly dyed purple punk hair, feeling vomity and regretful of whatever clumsy fumble I'd just escaped from with whichever silly insensitive stinky boy was game.

Anyhoo, you know what I mean. It's possible to reframe the grim, dark morning as a glamorous remnant of night. In fact, it's possible to realign almost any kind of thinking if you really want to. I have experimented with this very thing a few times in my life, and I have never once regretted it. It's when you decide to step to the side of your life for a moment to have a good look at it, almost like pulling in to a lay-by on a busy road. I try to give my eyes and ears and brain a few minutes off from the fast flow of life traffic and have a pit stop.

Sometimes, if you're lucky, it's blindingly obvious what changes need to happen if you can bring yourself to be brutally honest. Sometimes, of course, it's not, because you're either not ready to make any changes or don't want to or maybe even don't see them at all. The latter is normally the clearest sign of denial for me! On the lucky occasions that it's clear as day, I have to consciously decide to alter my mindset, usually about something I have long-held beliefs attached to. I can be remarkably stubborn, because, of course, it's much easier to carry on ploughing the same old familiar furrow, isn't it? Even if it's not straight and yields nothing.

A couple of years ago I came across a secret weapon that I keep in my arsenal, ready for use at a moment's notice if I sense that I am bedding down into the wrong mindset. It's this, a tiny, mighty poem by the American poet Jane Hirshfield:

'I moved my chair into sun

I sat in the sun

The way hunger is moved when called fasting.'

There. That's it. Boom. When I first read it, a depth charge went off inside me. The feeling you have when deep is calling to deep. When something is undeniably, universally true. Totally authentic. I had a seismic, visceral reaction somewhere in my limbic system, and I knew that I would certainly never forget it. Mainly because I needed it to help me right some tilted things back into position, things that had gone a bit skewy. I needed to move my 'chair' into sun, and I needed to sit there and notice the difference. Needed to let the sunlight drench me and realize what it's like to move your thinking, to reframe and reclaim your attitude, your reaction, your control. It's powerful stuff and, for me, it really works.

January is good for this. With last year firmly behind us we can properly resolve to make this year a blummin' good one. When I say good, I don't mean that I will measure the success of it by whether or not I have swum with dolphins or had a meaningful tattoo or learnt Chinese. I'm sure it's lovely to do any of those things, but I will be very happy with some smaller, more attainable achievements. If I am a degree more tolerant perhaps, or if I can mend a fractured friendship or tell a long-held truth or forgive that annoying twot, it would be big for me. I can only do those things, though, if I ACTIVELY change my thinking.

I know I can.

Will I?

The way to succeed at making change is, I suspect, to do it in incrementally small phases, so that it's possible and not too overwhelming. We all know how our good intentions positively kick us off at the beginning of the year. I can't count the amount of diaries I have crammed full with entries in January, that then fizzle out as the other months pile in. One of my teenage diaries has fulsome fizzing reports of every single conversation, thought and feeling about every friend, every crush, every journey, every meal, every argument, every family commitment, every appointment until mid-March, when the entry on March 18th simply reads,

'Washed hair.'

...Which is an achievement of sorts, I suppose, and better than 'didn't wash hair', but still...I don't want the bigness of the year ahead to upend me, or you, so I am reminding us both to go steady and think of it all in bite-size chunks. One thing at a time.

You have probably, in the last few weeks, been cajoled into making some resolutions. OH LORD, I HATE RESOLUTIONS. The giant dread of certain failure that accompanies them unlocks a fearful guilt in me. Not only do I predict that I won't be capable of sticking to the said resolution, but I am reminded of the tsunami of regret I have about all the previous let-downs. It's a spiral of disappointment.

So.

I'm not going to make resolutions.

BUT.

I AM going to have a small, manageable list of intentions in my back pocket. Something I may well look back at when the end of the year comes, just to have a sneaky peek at and consider whether I have gone anywhere near progress. If I haven't, so be it, I'm not going to beat myself up. I will simply know that they were in my thoughts, and that will just have to be good enough.

Here is my list of intentions for this year:

- make sure that wanting stuff doesn't allow me to forget what I already have
- do less catastrophizing
- be a bit quiet and not mind if I sometimes feel a bit sad, even if I don't know why
- be honest if I find someone/something fake – I need authenticity at all times
- be wary of folk who don't take responsibility for their actions
- notice and identify my insecurities, so that I can tackle them honestly
- donate to a new charity anonymously
- make more time for family stuff
- make cake
- drink less coffee
- walk more
- kiss for longer

That's probably enough, although I can think of thousands more.

But I want to keep it realistic and possible. I reckon I might manage those and I know for sure that I want to, so . . . let's see.

In a funny way, there's a real thrill in the uncertainty of having a whole new year ahead. Possibility is potent. I have wonderful little lightbulb moments when I believe that I'm capable of anything, and they occur most frequently at the dawn of the year, right here in January. It's like my courage is at its most fully charged. I'm right at the top of the year and I can see a long way ahead, and it looks inviting. There, in the distance, is a mountain, a big dark-blue mountain, and I really, really want to get there. I'm not entirely sure what's at the top of it, but I'm drawn to it and I want to try to make sure that my decisions and my actions take me closer to it. It's a ways away, but it's within my reach, it's my horizon, and I'm going to do my best to get there. So long as I'm trying, I'm satisfied, thanks. I might need rests and refreshments along the way, but my face is forever turned towards it.

The main thing that could prevent me from stepping forward is a tendency I have to fold myself away. S'funny, isn't it? For a person who has spent a great deal of her life in groups or partnerships, on stage, in front of a camera etc., I am actually a relatively reserved creature. Maybe it's not strange at all. Maybe it's classic. All of us need a bit of peace and quiet now and then, but I reckon I would make a very happy hermit. With the exception of extensive visiting rights for beloveds. I am most comfortable in my own company, but equally I need to be part of my tribe of family and friends. That tight group can be quite surprisingly small, I realize. I don't need many, just the inner sanctum of those I properly know, love and trust. They know who they are. For them, EVERYTHING and ANYTHING of me is available, anytime, anyhow, up, down, in, out and sideways. I will NEVER run out of whatever it is they need of me, I will always be there and I will fight to kill on their behalf. I'm not afraid to bite. I'm not afraid of monsters or pirates. Or Americans. I take my role inside this bubble very seriously, be it wife, mum, stepmum, sister, daughter-in-law, sister-in-law, best friend, cousin, niece, wife of gay husband or close friend. If I am your any of the above, you have direct access to my heart and soul with no filters, barriers or prerequisites. I am going to forgive any of your mistakes or insensitivities. I am going to be your advocate. I am going to listen to you. I am going to try to understand you. I am going to get alongside you so that you never feel alone. I will endeavour to never misuse you. I am going to assume that we are equal, but I am going to respect our differences. (Unless of course, they involve chocolate, in which case I will always be selfish, greedy and violent.) I am going to love you so hard you may well beg for mercy and release. Which I will NOT grant. Resistance is futile.

Look, the fact is that like most of us, I value the time to unmuddle my thoughts. Otherwise I can't be emotionally fit enough for what lies ahead. I won't even get to the foothills of my mountain. I am trying to learn that if I could just embrace the uncertainty of the future, if I could find it exciting, if I worried less, life would be a more simple journey. I so wish I could more easily be impetuous, but I'm always high in the tree, on the lookout, one eye on danger, one eye on the mountain. Hopefully that doesn't mean that my eyes are looking two different ways …it's not an attractive look. Mind you, it never hurt Marty Feldman.

All I really mean is that here in January, I am hoping I will remember and maintain this lovely confident feeling of intent and faith in the future. High hopes are good.

I want to remember, all year, that I can move my chair into sun at any point. I can reframe anything if it helps me to live better. I can decide that this is going to be a good year concerning ANYTHING that I control. In other words, anything that comes from me, from my heart, from my mind, from my mouth. There are, of course, various things that come from other more challenging and personal parts of me that I simply can't control, and long may that be the case.

So, with a fair wind (!) behind us, come on this year, here we go, I can see the tip of the mountain in the distance.

I am:

- A female
- A mother
- A wife
- A stepmother
- A sister
- A friend
- A Susan
- Self-employed
- Short, apparently
- Bossy
- A boss
- A writer
- A mammal
- Punctual
- A show-off
- Anchored
- A Luddite
- A grandmother-in-waiting

- A great kisser
- Lost without my diary
- All right on my own
- A wanker
- A Quaker
- A Quaker wanker
- A dog lover
- A tip-top driver
- A client
- An art collector
- A dancer
- A person of the eighties
- A reluctant flyer
- A consummate nosey parker
- A supreme twot
- The one and only, nobody I'd rather be*

*I'm not, Chesney Hawkes is, you idiot.

Now you ...

- _____
- _____
- _____
- _____
- _____
- _____
- _____
- _____
- _____
- _____
- _____
- _____
- _____
- _____
- _____
- _____

JANUARY

monday »

tuesday »

wednesday »

thursday »

friday »

saturday »

sunday »

JANUARY

monday »

tuesday »

wednesday »

thursday »

friday »

saturday »

sunday »

JANUARY

monday »

tuesday »

wednesday »

thursday »

friday »

saturday »

sunday »

JANUARY

monday »

tuesday »

wednesday »

thursday »

friday »

saturday »

sunday »

JANUARY

monday »

tuesday »

wednesday »

thursday »

friday »

saturday »

sunday »

Would-be Valentines

1. **George Clooney**

   Pros: Good jaw. Piercing eyes. Makes you feel like you're the only one in the room. Funny.
   Cons: Amal is clever, beautiful and we really like her.

2. **Idris Elba**

   Pros: Arms that go right round. Twinkly handsomeness. Calming bedtime stories voice.
   Cons: Too popular with other girls. Too many dangerous speedy/fighty hobbies combined with too many white T-shirts to maintain.

3. **Frank Sinatra**

   Pros: He's got me under his skin. Well connected.
   Cons: Too small. Is dead.

4. **Emma Willis**

   Pros: Great hair so I can share/steal products. Smells lovely (I imagine).
   Cons: Too tall in heels.

5. **Nigel Farage**

   Pros: None.
   Cons: Infinite.

I've started this list, you finish it.

6. ....

    Pros: ....

    Cons: ....

7. ....

    Pros: ....

    Cons: ....

8. ....

    Pros: ....

    Cons: ....

9. ....

    Pros: ....

    Cons: ....

10. ....

    Pros: ....

    Cons: ....

FEBRUARY

By now any worthy intentions I had in the New Year about eating less, better, healthier, have pretty much fizzled out and I am having that interesting internal dialogue which goes like this:

Deluded Me: Oh damn, I've forgotten to have a mind for my physical well-being and my lips just accidentally fell on to a deep-pan pizza . . .

Very Deluded Me: That's fine, because it's still sort of Winter, and we all need extra blubber to keep out the cold, don't we? Even cavemen knew that. Otherwise I will DIE.

Deluded Me: Yeah, but I have central heating . . . so I'm not entirely relying on body hair and fat to keep me warm, if we're honest.

Very Deluded Me: Hmmn, maybe . . . but there's also the added thing which is that, unlike every other human woman, I tend to look better and yes, even feel better, the fatter I am. So. Please just pass the clotted cream, please, and thank you.

Very Very Deluded Me: Oh yes, I'd forgotten just how great I can look if I just bother to put more effort into eating lard and treacle. I mustn't be so darn lazy, I must walk to the fridge more often. And to avoid that freezing to death outside option, I really must mainly sit down, inside, on a sofa watching telly and ridding the world of chocolate.

(APPLAUSE AND WHOOPS OF APPROVAL FROM ALL DELUDED PARTIES.)

Now, If I am not careful to remain inside my confidence forcefield, this sort of nonsense can become a persuasive loud and destructive voice, so extra effort at positive thinking has to kick in. I was once lucky enough to be on Graham Norton's couch with the divine alabaster goddess that is Nicole Kidman. She is a tall woman and she was wearing high heels, so when we were backstage, I found myself mainly conversing with her fanny, since that's what was at eye level. I'm not complaining, all of her is perfectly lovely, it's just that when I'm next to such a wonderfully long woman, I can feel quite small in lots of ways. In front of the camera, I invited her to stand up so that I could show the audience the difference. At moments like this, I often imagine what it would be like if aliens landed right at that very moment.

'Hello, aliens, and welcome. Let me take this opportunity to demonstrate the marvellous diversity of what we like to call WOMEN. Both of the specimens in front of you are women. Both contain brains and organs and bones and reproductive systems (some are modified) and digestive systems and eyes and a heart and fannies and bumholes and blood and everything that makes us work. It's just that one of us contains all of this stuff in the same amount of space that the other one has for only her legs. Just legs. Legs as long as the short one is tall. Amazing, isn't it? Yet one is no better than the other in any way ... except perhaps one can see more at a football game, but otherwise these two creatures are utterly EQUAL. Imagine that.'

I had exactly the same experience of utter wonderment when I was doing a *French and Saunders* sketch which included the phenomenon that is Darcey Bussell. It was a silly ballet sketch, so she was in a leotard, which of course displayed every contour of her wonderful lithe body. I couldn't take my eyes off her to the point of rude, creepy staring. I couldn't, and still can't, imagine living inside a long bendy body like that. Being that high up and so graceful as you are transported around your world atop lengthy, lean, muscular legs, looking over hedges and seeing the tops of people's heads, what might that be like? Imagine the ground you can cover at speed with such a long stride? Imagine being able to reach anything on a top shelf? Imagine crossing your legs and then having enough leg left to tuck your foot in behind your other leg? Imagine that!

Mind you, I do as much imagining about all sorts of other bodies, especially men's. Imagine having broad shoulders and no bosoms and all that untidiness in your front pants? Imagine being in a 100-year-old body? Or a baby's body? Or a one-legged person's body? Or an athlete's body? Or a one-legged athlete's body? Or a cat's body ...?

Here I am though, permanently ensconced in this strange little body my parents gifted me. The only body I truly know. When I look down at it from the top, it's quite an interesting sight because pretty much all I see is bosoms and the ground below with the tips of my feet poking out. It's not a great angle really, but remember, it's not the view of your body that anyone else gets, it's only from YOUR head. The front-on view they see is much more flattering and, actually, more accurate.

When I think of all the pointless hours I spent, especially as a younger teenager, wishing my body was different, I feel quite sad. Me ol' mate and erstwhile comedy partner Jennifer and I were talking about this, and we decided to root out pictures of when we remembered being the most unhappy about our physical selves. What we saw, of course, were two young girls, aged about fourteen, who are bloody gorgeous, and, like so many girls of that age, who have no clue that they are perfectly lovely just as they are. Maybe you're not supposed to be too confident at this age, maybe you're supposed to waver and wobble and fret but ... blimey ... why?! As if you don't have enough challenges on your plate! When do we learn to beat ourselves up so badly about our bodies? Is it at school? Is it about comparison? Is it when that unwinnable battle begins between the desire to be unique versus wanting so desperately to fit in? Why is doubt so resolutely the referee? And fear the only true victor?

Luckily my dad gave me armour in those tricky formative years, and because of that I reckon I'm reasonably confident about how my body is, but I still have misgivings that I reckon are fairly universal. Let me run you through them as I see them, starting with:

HEAD

Yep, relatively happy with this. Inherited most of this area directly from my parents. My hair is quite thick, and keeps my head warm. Just a quick moment about hair: why is it so important? How the hell would we explain it to those same aliens that landed when I was standing next to Nicole Kidman? 'Yes, it's thousands of strands of dead stuff that hangs off our heads and we spend thousands of money, probably hundreds per strand, in our lifetime, making sure we regularly cut it off and paint it to be a different colour. Yes, you may well tilt your big green bald MEKON head quizzically ...' For some inexplicable reason, I feel fortunate to have plenty of hair to be constantly cutting and colouring. It's bonkers.

I have ears, eyes, nose and mouth that all seem to function pretty well. Five of those are actual holes in my body ... which is weird when you think about it. And on that, sorry to digress, but exactly how many holes do we believe a woman has? Excluding eyeballs and skin pores of course, it would just be silly to include those. I've done a quick tally, and personally I think it's eight, but some do say seven. Look, discuss it with your gynaecologist and draw your own conclusions. I'm not really that bothered about the accuracy, I've decided it's all part of a woman's mystery, y'know: 'I am woman, I am many, many holes, I am a colander, I am a golf course, I am Emmental cheese ...'

Anyway, anyway, back to **HEAD**. Most of my face is arranged in a fairly symmetrical pattern. Obviously it's crinkling with age, but that's to be expected, and I think a corrugated face is quite useful for rain guttering.

NECK

Well, this is of course irrelevant, as I don't have one. Nope. No-Neck-Nancy, that's me. Everyone in my family goes directly from chin to chest without passing GO. No inward curvature whatsoever. More convex, like a gobble on a rooster. This does lead to various jewellery crises because I have been informed that a necklace belongs, apparently . . . on a neck. I have no neck. Therefore I have no necklace. No bitterness there . . . move along to . . .

SHOULDERS

Where, obviously, I keep my chips. My shoulders are not really much use, to be honest, except to keep my bra straps on, and they're useful for shrugging, but nothing really to see here.

ARMS

Yes, these are really quite interesting. They're definitely much shorter than is required. They are basically a couple of butchers' wives stocky leg o'muttons. They're not pretty, not elegant. I can't pull off strappy dresses, but they ARE fit for purpose. They carry stuff, they go around kids and friends, and a husband's neck, so I'm OK with that.

HANDS

Right, yes. The extreme of my body, five cocktail sausages flopping about at the end there, quite untidy really. I have had them described as 'stumpy' before now, but seriously how blummin' amazing are they? In terms of sheer engineering they're phenomenal. There are twenty-seven bones in each one, and they are the densest area of nerve endings in our whole body. And what about the whole opposable thumb thing, that lets me know I'm a primate? Fantastic. It's all the things I've DONE with these hands that matter most to me:

- I held my mum and dad's hands with them
- I held my daughter's hand
- I played two ball at the garage wall for hours
- I've stood on them
- I've held on tight at fairgrounds
- I've slapped an idiot's cheek
- I've shaken Fatty Saunders' hand every show night
- I've had my future told from them (rubbish, charlatan)
- I've pinched and punched my brother with them
- I've put wedding rings on the left one (twice!)
- I've measured ponies with them
- I've trained dogs with them
- I've cooked pasties with them
- I've cradled genitals
- I've clicked and clapped to Madonna on stage live
- I've touched a dolphin
- I've been in some soft, secret places (see above)
- I've pointed like MAD

So basically, everything I've ever touched has been touched by these hands of mine. EVERYTHING. That means every single piece of chocolate I've ever eaten has been placed in my cakehole by these very hands. Oh, THANK YOU, hands.

NORKS/BOSOMS/BAPS

Little and Large, Wood and Walters . . . or, if I'm furious with them, and I often am because they're such show-offs, ANT and DEC. My boobs pretty much arrive everywhere before I do. They even arrived on my body before I was ready. I can't remember a time when I wasn't lugging them around. I once took my bra off on a radio show and put it on my head, thereby proving that my entire head fits into ONE CUP of my 42G industrial bra. So I am carrying around two whole-head-sized lumps on my front. Frankly, it's astonishing that I remain upright at all. So, yes, OK, they're fairly big, and wayhayhay and phwoar and all of that, but y'know, calm down, what are they really? Just some udders that boys regard as a theme park.

BELLY

Now then. Something interesting here. I am the only person I know who has a belly the exact same size and in the exact same position on the FRONT of my body, as my arse is on the BACK. How did THAT happen?!

Why am I asking you? I know EXACTLY how it happened – CURLY WURLYS. That's how. So, I am, in actuality, a sphere, a barrel. With legs. Like a sort of human M&M character. Is that a good thing or a bad thing? Do I really mind? In truth I don't consider it that much. If my belly doesn't fit my trousers, I get bigger trousers. OF COURSE I know it's good to be aware of health risks, but come on, what is life without a Curly Wurly every now and then?

GROWLER

The GROTTO OF MANY BEGUILING DELIGHTS, the LADYGARDEN, or as I prefer to call mine . . . Mumford & Sons . . . (y'know, the beardy ones). Nothing much I really want to share about this particular area of mine (I can hear the collective sigh of relief), except to say that the entire environs, the complete service station, is marvellous. Thank you.

HIPS

I like my hips very much. At least the bits that I think are generally regarded as hips. I'm not entirely sure exactly where they are to be honest, but I think it's the part that moves most when any Shakira music comes on. Talking of which, I once overdanced so severely to 'Hips Don't Lie' that I actually injured my actual hip. I had to walk with a stick for six weeks. So frankly, Shakira love, your hips DO lie.

LEGS

I was clearly given someone else's.

These ones are a short, fat, elderly MAN'S legs.

By elderly, I mean dead.

My legs are not for a woman.

Once, Fatty Saunders and I did a sketch where we had to be hoicked up on wires for hours on end. When you do that, they put you in a special flying harness. Hers was a tiny little dainty nylon one. Mine arrived in a trunk. It was a big leather strappy monstrosity/sling type of thing that you might lift a horse in. As I was climbing into the heavy-duty truss, I saw the name tag etched on the inside of the strap, the person it had originally been made for. Harry Secombe. Don't get me wrong. I LOVED Harry. But really? I have HIS body? Yes. I have Harry Secombe's legs. Thank you, God. Not.

FEET

Mine are those of a hobbit. They're fuzzy and don't fit any ordinary-width shoes. But they carry me about year after year and rarely complain, so I'm happy with that.

That's it, basically. That's how I see my body. It does its job, it's healthy and I like it. Even though some of it is a bit strange and it doesn't fit very well on any scientific chart, and it doesn't match up to any 'ideal'. It's never stopped me doing anything I want to do.

It's where I live, and I fit in it very comfortably, thank you.

But . . . it's just my shell.

It's not the only thing that defines me.

So when and if anyone tries to bully me or any other woman because of the way our bodies are, my blood boils. There might be choices we make in our lives that could entail shame, yes, but intimating that ANYONE should feel shame because of their body is not OK by me. Look at those evil red rings of shame that certain women's magazines highlight people's supposed flaws with? Only a bully would do this purposely, point out a mistake or blemish with glee like that. It's so unkind.

Why not do the opposite? Why not help us to build our fragile confidence by pointing out the LOVELY parts instead? Give us something to emulate and admire. We don't need all the crushing, ta. Allow us to learn to accept and be content with how we look. Let us take a few less selfies (self included) and begin to look outwards a bit more. Let us let ourselves off the hook more often. Let us age naturally if we want to and celebrate that process for the gift it is. Let us acknowledge that people come in all kinds of shapes and sizes and let us enjoy that by making clothes that FIT EVERYONE, and by focusing on what's fantastic about all of us instead of what's found wanting.

Bugger that. Bugger regret and self-hatred. I'm going to take the risk of actually liking myself, flaws 'n' all, and see where that leads me. I have this one earthly life only. Am I really going to spend the majority of it hating myself?

Bugger that!

Feel free to put red rings around the parts
of your body that you LOVE...

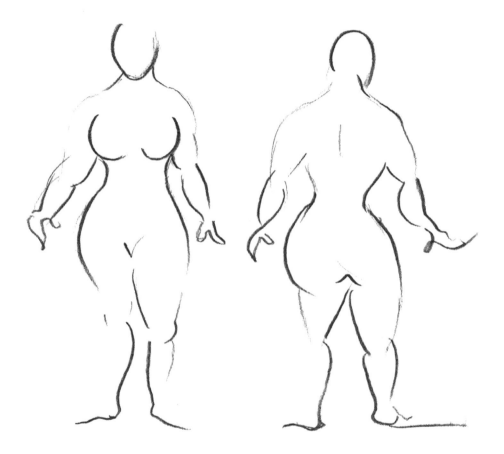

FEBRUARY

monday »

tuesday »

wednesday »

thursday »

friday »

saturday »

sunday »

FEBRUARY

monday »

tuesday »

wednesday »

thursday »

friday »

saturday »

sunday »

FEBRUARY

monday »

tuesday »

wednesday »

thursday »

friday »

saturday »

sunday »

FEBRUARY

monday »

tuesday »

wednesday »

thursday »

friday »

saturday »

sunday »

FEBRUARY

monday »

tuesday »

wednesday »

thursday »

friday »

saturday »

sunday »

Place another picture of yourself here, as you are right now.

SPRING

The engine is Spring, the fuel is beauty. All of those resolutions promised in the sleepy grip of New Year's wintery fug can now be realized, because we have a new gear to throttle forward into.

There are all kinds of budding and blossoming and buzzing happening everywhere. Birds, animals and plants unfurl, unfold and burst into life. Look at it all:

- swallows and herons and wrens and skylarks
- toads and adders and lambs and butterflies
- daffodils and primroses and crocuses and violets
- wild garlic and hawthorn

and lovely lovely snowdrops, which always indicate the return of Spring. 'Our Lady of February' the early Catholics called them in monastery gardens. My granny called them 'Fair Maids of February'. I call them snowdrops.

The grass is just that bit greener, the blue sky is proper BIG blue, all the colours gather strength, and the wonderful light just promises EVERYTHING, doesn't it? Somehow it's so . . . hopeful. It's all a bit sexy. Even the toads. No wonder there's a Spring in our step!

More and more as I grow older, I come to realize that we are bound to the seasons in so many ways. Even climate change hasn't altered that in any significant way. Yet.

Being aware that so many seasons have ebbed and flowed ages before us, and will continue to do so ages after us, serves to remind us how held we are by them, how inevitable they are. How quickly time trickles past.

Our lives are really seasons too, in the bigger sense. Our lifespan chimes with them. Spring is the first twenty-five years, Summer is twenty-five to fifty years, Autumn is fifty to seventy-five years and Winter is seventy-five to … well … the end, the forever end.

So, Spring is the beginning really, the birth, the very start of life. From babyhood, through infancy, that whole first lap into our mid-twenties, such a hugely formative part of our story. This is the abundant time. When life gives us so much, when we have to think and feel so quickly because time is galloping on. These are the years when life is happening TO us, it's later that we get the chance to consider it and wrestle it into shape. From zero to twenty-five years, we are receptors. That's why I believe that massive luck comes into play. It's luck if you find yourself in a loving family, if your parents stay together, if no-one bullies you or hurts you or makes you feel small, if you live in a safe country, if you have good teachers, if you don't experience the early death of someone you love, if you make enduring friendships, if you have grandparents, if you have good health, if you have good eyesight, if you enjoy your own company, if you don't have wide hobbit-like feet, if your hair doesn't fall out … just luck. There's pretty much nothing you can do about any of the above and yet they prescribe a large part of how you turn out. It don't seem fair.

For me, it's obvious that the biggest part of who we become is … who really made us. We are made of everyone around us when we are little, and we are shaped by who we choose to have around us when we are adults. I look at who made me, and although I stand short and steady like a Weeble here in my own shoes today, I walk in the footsteps of all who went before me. Mainly family, but also friends. I am made of all of them. Even the dodgy ones.

Here's my list of key players:

GOOD GRANNY MARJORIE

A tiny woman made entirely of cake and powerful, unquestionable goodness. She taught ballroom dancing in her youth and had a phenomenal collection of dolls in her loft. Dolls from all around the world, in national dress, all colours and sizes. Some had eyes that shut. All had pants, because if they arrived without, she'd make some to preserve their dignity. Granny hadn't travelled, but the dolls had. Us grandchildren cuddled up to her in the warm bed in her cold front bedroom to have stories. There was a Camberwick spread on the bed and condensation dripping down the window. She wore size 3 shoes. Some were gold and had a heel for dancing. I could fit into them perfectly when I was about nine. It was THRILLING. She was the only family member other than my bro and mum that I told about the adoption of my daughter, because she was the most TRUSTWORTHY person I ever knew. I felt safe and loved around her, and she taught me how to be a grand-daughter. I will always, always miss her.

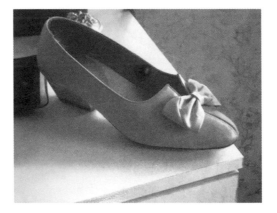

EVIL GRANNY LILLIAN

Known to our side of the family as 'Fag Ash Lil'. She was a handful, a tricky ol' broad with a colourful history, a sharp tongue and a short fuse. She loved rabbit-skin fur coats, sparkly bling and clacky shoes. She loved gin and arcades and the British Legion and bookies and darts. I often slept in the same room as her when I was a child, on what she called the 'cot' (a pull-out bed). She would leave her teeth in a glass on her bedside table overnight and set an alarm to wake her at intervals so that she could drink from a flask in the night. She SAID it was water ...

She showed me how to play cards and she taught me not to be ashamed of, or deny, our working-class background. She had a formidable eff-off attitude that I admired, though could never quite emulate. She wasn't the most naturally maternal of women, but that didn't have to matter to me because she wasn't MY mother. For me, she was as bold as brass, ballsy and fearless, a consummate survivor.

MY DAD

He took his own life when I was nineteen, so my memories of him are limited to only those nineteen years. I feel cheated I didn't know him adult to adult. Mind you, do we ever know our parents as such, I wonder? Perhaps we are always stuck in the amber of the child–parent relationship to some extent. I CERTAINLY am when it comes to him. Such an important significant, influential person in my life ... ripped away just as I might have been starting to understand him. I realize that I lionize him to some extent. I don't care. He gave me that armour of confidence by reminding me often how much I mattered and how beautiful I was in his eyes. When you're a curious little dumpy girl, your dad's eyes are the main ones you see yourself reflected in. They are your mirror, and in that mirror I saw and believed I was bloody gorgeous. I knew, because he told me, that I was NOT to accept second best when it came to boys, that I was NOT to be grateful for their attentions, that I was deserving of kindness, humour and respect, that I was a prize worth cherishing, that I absolutely

knew how to love another, because look how well I loved my family. He told me to protect my reputation and my dignity. He told me I was truly, resolutely, undeniably loved. And I knew it to be fact. I knew it in my blood and bones, and no-one could ever persuade me otherwise. Not ever.

Here's a thing I know FOR SURE, and something we need to tell all the dads. Know this, and be in NO doubt about it, your daughters, your darling daughters, will measure every significant male in their lives by you. So, sorry to say it, but you'd better be a tip-top enough example of a proper man. Be someone to aspire to. Be decent and kind and cheerful and understanding and generous and funny and selfless. No pressure then ...

My dad was a gentle chap, a bit too sensitive for the macho world he inhabited, I suspect. He was easily embarrassed in the company of those he didn't know so well, but at home he was certainly not. He was funny and silly. Interesting, considering the fact that from the age of sixteen, and most likely before, he suffered crippling depression, and in a time when it was shameful to have such an illness he, of course, attempted to hide it. From colleagues, friends, family, and, I guess, from himself. I didn't know my dad was mentally unwell. I knew he had bouts of 'migraine' and took to his bed with 'piles'. We would sometimes tiptoe about the house so as not to wake him if he was in a darkened room, 'getting some rest'. I didn't know he was in seven kinds of hell at those times, fighting off the black dogs that were ravaging him.

His suicide imploded our family and drenched us in sadness. That is undeniable and a massive part of my history . . . BUT, here's the more important thing . . . we SURVIVED it. Ironically, I think one of the reasons our little four-sided square of a family became a strong, solid triangle after he was gone was because of him, and all he taught us about how to look after each other. That's exactly what we did, right from the off, from the dark minute when we discovered what he'd done, that awful minute, so pitifully different to the minute before . . . when we had a dad. A lovely dad.

So there I was, aged nineteen, having had a childhood full of safety, nurture and plenty of adventures, teetering on the edge of adulthood and loaded with grief. All I knew was that, true to the memory of my dad, I needed to step forward. Just like when he taught me to swim as a nipper living in Cyprus, where he was posted with the RAF. I was six when we moved there, and as so much time was spent by the sea, I really needed to know how to swim. He coaxed me into the water, deeper and deeper. He caught me when I leapt from rocks into the darker blue water. Never once did I think he wouldn't catch me. He was the one holding me carefully when I discovered that if you kick like this and that and flail this way and that, you do eventually remain buoyant, you breathe, you swim, you survive. Very quickly I wanted a snorkel and flippers. I sorta believed I had gills. I spent hours under the water, closely inspecting the phenomenon of magnified skin pores on the back of my hand, my toes, sand, rocks, fish. All of it was wondrous. The regular sound of my own breathing underwater through the amplification of the plastic breathing tube was comforting and became the soundtrack of my private, splendid submarine life. I had no fear.

Above water is equally exhilarating, because that's where hours and pruney-skin-hours of delight happen when Dad pretends to be my own personal dolphin, whilst I hang around his neck and he speeds through the water faster than any human surely can. How strong and broad and brown are his shoulders and how lovely is it to feel the water splashing on my face? How safe do I feel when he tosses me in the air and I splash into the water nearby only to be scooped up by my dolphin dad who is, by now, even making the required dolphin noises?!

However cruelly short my time was with my father – after all it only existed in the Spring of my life – it couldn't have been more potent. I remember so much, and it all sticks. I try to live my life as a tribute to him. I always have him with me, as my energy and my engine. I go steady. Left foot. Right foot. Breathe.

If there can be anything learnt from such a disaster, it is this for me – it's really OK to fail. Nothing in life should matter so much that it trumps our will to live. Let's risk failure and be as brave as we can for as long as we can. And let's choose to live.

MY MUM

Of course, literally made me.

I started like a lot of us, as a baby. A red-spotted lump of a baby, with scarlet fever, apparently. My two-year-old brother thought Mum had given birth to a giant screaming strawberry. It was a lengthy, complicated birth, Mum liked to remind me. She also wanted me to know that in those days of poor dental care, little info about calcium, and no fluoride in the water, she donated her top teeth to my bro, and her bottom teeth to me. When I think about it now, how strange it must have been to have entirely false and ill-fitting teeth from your twenties onwards.

There was a rod of steel running right down my mum's spine. Although she suffered plenty of self-doubt, she was pretty much fearless and tackled everything head-on. Sometimes she was so caught up in her valour, she lost sight of how audacious she might have become on occasion. She was a ferocious advocate for the underdog. A powerhouse. Extremely loving but quite strict. You would want her on your team. A monster love truck with eight reserve tanks if you should have need of them, plenty for everyone.

A working-class woman, she always felt that she was being looked down on, and so she shook off her natural West Country burr and adopted a faux posh Mrs Bouquet-type accent. I think lots of people did that in the fifties, there was a kind of received pronunciation of the Queen's English that newsreaders and broadcasters used, and that was the ideal. Occasionally, usually when ruddy angry, Mum would slip up and we would hear her familiar Plymouth accent flood back. Both she and my dad were born and raised there. Janners, we call 'em, and proud.

Since Dad was in the RAF and consequently our family were regularly moved around the country and abroad to different bases, Mum had to find work wherever we ended up. She re-invented herself so many times, adapting and surviving at every turn. She was a serial truth-shifter, re-telling and re-framing situations to suit her purpose and her moral compass.

I loved the smell of her and, though she's been gone nigh on five years, I can still summon it if I close my eyes and conjure her up. It's a mixture of stew, lily of the valley, smoke, washing powder, coffee, bosoms and pasties. Unmistakably Mum.

GARY

Those are the folk who taught me how to be a granddaughter and a daughter, and it was Gary who taught me how to be a sister. Having an older brother is a blessing and a curse when you're younger, for both of you. He once beat up some boys who threatened to pull my pants down when I was five, so I always knew he had my back. On the other hand, he did regularly pin me down with his knees on my shoulders and dribble on my face. He did also explain to me on various occasions throughout our childhood that I was the only person he could gleefully actually murder, and I think he may have had good reason. I knew full well how to annoy him and, inexplicably, I couldn't stop myself doing those very things AD NAUSEAM until I wound him up tighter than a coiley-coiled coil, then I would stand back, watch him explode and then loudly complain to Mum and Dad that he had shouted at me. Evil little sis, born to torture him. The fact is, throughout our entire lives we have looked out for each other, as taught by Dad, and to this day, he is the first person I call when big stuff happens. He has known me my WHOLE LIFE, every living minute of it. Not only has he known me, he knows me, and I really know him. He is my blood and I love the bones of him and his family. Plus – he's a great dad, so for me, that means he's a great man.

Safe in the surety of the love of these five, my passage through childhood into spotty young adulthood was pretty smooth. I didn't realize that the relative plain-sailing was in actuality a chance for me to load up my knapsack of confidence in readiness for the tornado that would buffet us all when Dad died. On reflection, I now know that all the life provisions that were carefully, thoughtfully packed away in those early years are what have provided me with sustenance ever since.

Every positive experience, however small and everyday it may seem, is another unit of provisions for the knapsack, which gets fuller and heavier. You never mind carrying it if it's chock-full o' good stuff. In fact the weight helps to remind you of it, of what family feels like, of what shared responsibility and mutual concern are. Oh, Mum and Dad are laughing – I'll have that. Now they're kissing – have that. Now they are arguing – not sure if I want that. Oh I see, now they're making up and forgiving each other – yep, I'll have that. They're teasing me – I'll have that. We're all going to see the latest James Bond film together – definitely have that. We're singing Beatles songs in the car – yep. And on, and on . . . Unfortunately, the opposite is also true of course. That knapsack can be very heavy indeed if it's full of hurt and shame and anger. So heavy, in fact, that it can prevent you from moving forward, it can drag you to the ground and collapse you.

The learning is happening in such huge dollops in these early years, it's easy to be overwhelmed and consequently make tons of mistakes. Of course. There's no problem with that so long as you can recognize that's what they are. That's ALL they are. You are young, it's all reversible, all salvageable. No guilt necessary. Little do we know that actually, in this strangely elastic stage of our youth, we are forming our own template over which we will trace many moments of our lives thereafter, honing and adjusting all the time, altering the settings.

Does time pass differently in these formative years? I'm only thinking of the lazy, long, long summers right next to the yearly birthdays that seem to occur every other week, too fast, too fast.

For some, those years of birth to twenty-five contain babyhood, school, college (or not), relationships, work, marriage and babyhood again (or not). A whole huge cycle happens. It's in these years that our passions are fierce, our bodies are ripe, we believe we are invincible and we KNOW we are RIGHT. Why on earth wouldn't we make tons of mahoosive decisions? Yes, I will get engaged at nineteen. Yes, I will have a tight curly perm. Yes, I will have careless sex with an entirely unsuitable boy without a condom and worry myself sick for six weeks. Yes, I will spend more money than I earn on a piece of Monty Don jewellery and get into big, fat debt.

And anyway, this is when we are asked to make choices. We are constantly measured and when we are sixteen, we are expected to decide our workplace future by beginning the cull of subjects that we may not excel at. We start to focus on who we think we are and who we might turn out to be. If we are very lucky, these choices will be nearly right. If we are even luckier, those older and wiser around us will remind us that they too are still trying to work it out and that any possibly misguided choices made at this lovely young age can be rectified anytime later.

OK to try.
OK to make mistakes.
OK to not know.
OK to try again.
OK to make better mistakes.
OK to know a tiny bit more.

It's Spring. The sap is rising. The buds are opening. It's a time for HOPE and OPTIMISM. Pull your knapsack on tight and bring it on . . .

Four People Who, When You First Met, You Didn't Realize Would Become So Important To You:

1. **The BF**

   I met her at drama college, training as teachers, forty years ago, when I operated the lights for her final exam production. We fell in love. There is NOTHING about me that she doesn't know. We are the very best of friends, we share an unbreakable bond, and she is the custodian of my heart.

2. **The Gay Husband**

   We met at a youth theatre company when we were fourteen years old. Inseparable ever since. All others shall not pass without his scrupulous approval. The best, cleverest, bitchiest laughs.

3. **The Comedy Partner**

   We were forced to share a flat together against both our wishes. Initial allergy to each other transformed into an irresistible magnetic force field, and craving for shared mischief. A beauty and a mensch.

4. **Alison Moyet**

   I flirt-danced with her in awe from across the room at a party in the early eighties. I didn't know she would fill my blood up with unconditional love and support for ever after. Always understanding. Never judging. Wise old head.

Now, your four people:

1. ....

2. ....

3. ....

4. ....

· ·

MARCH

When I think of March, I think of mothers. Mother's Day. Bounty and beauty.

Becoming a mum became a huge goal for me, because it didn't happen easily. Now let's get one thing clear right from the off. I'm not someone who believes that being a mother is the sole purpose of being a woman. I detest that women who have chosen not to, or maybe can't, have kids, are constantly judged so harshly, and in many cases by, of all people, other women, who should know better. Reproducing isn't a competition or proof of value or worth. It isn't a failure not to do so. We surely mustn't measure a person by the activities of their womb? How small-minded would that be? Plenty of women – of people – simply don't want to make children. That's just fine. I do have a problem, however, with people who actively dislike children.

Now.

Those people I take issue with. Or more likely, I would avoid. I suspect we wouldn't have much in common. We may not all choose to have children, but ALL of us raise them, whether we like it or not. If you are breathing, you are an example . . . of something, of someone, and children are watching and learning from every choice you make. They belong to our world and we were here before them, so we ought to explain our legacy and do the handover properly.

Anyhoo. A little rant there. Where was I? Oh yes, mothers. The incontrovertible fact is, we ALL had one. Some would say that the love of a mother, if you are fortunate enough to have it, is the purest and most unconditional love any of us will ever know. It's where science and love combine in the most mighty way, forging a bond strong enough to withstand giant adversity. The open, innocent trusting faith that almost every child places in their mother right from the very start is massively touching.

I'm not saying that fatherhood isn't as important, just that, as I see it, it's entirely different. Where else in life do we experience such an enduring connection? Even if we go through phases of actively disliking our mothers (I know I certainly did), they, the mothers, are still there, to remind us of our very nascence.

She conceived you.
She grew you inside her.
She delivered you.
She is your origin. You lived there. Right there.
Like it or not, she is the root of you. You are made of her.

Now, that doesn't mean you ARE her. Certainly not, God forbid, but yes, you started there. My body refused to co-operate in the baby-making department, or more accurately, our bodies refused. It's so easy to jump to conclusions when a couple are going through the pain of infertility. I remember so many instances where friends and family assumed the problem lay solely with me. I think this is because if a man has fertility issues it is seen as somehow speaking to the very heart of his manhood, and no-one dares, whereas women are . . . what? Tougher? Less sensitive? It's rot, of course. Our doc explained that in most cases both people in the couple have issues, sometimes simultaneously, sometimes not, so it's commonly quite difficult to simplify it and know exactly which one is culpable at any given moment. It's chemistry, biology, and fate having a row in a petri dish. They come to an agreement, but you don't get to find out what it is until weeks later when the brawl continues into your womb.

It was a difficult, testing time, just when our marriage was at its most fresh and exciting, this nagging low-level longing crept in. It was like my belly was calling to me to be a mother, one of the most certain and powerful urges I'd ever felt. And it kept relentlessly not happening.

And I wondered why it didn't work?

I even wondered if perhaps we weren't supposed to have a child; if it was somehow deemed that we shouldn't?

Then, with IVF, miraculously it DID work.

Then, within a few weeks, it didn't.

Big grief. More scans. More injections.

We started to dilute our happiness with this giant sadness.

We kept it all quiet, private.

So, chirpy normal life was going on all around.

Unaware.

Normal life, like when your friend gets pregnant by accident.

And you go with her for her abortion.

And you don't know if you love her or hate her.

And NONE of it is fair.

But then . . .

You work out that OF COURSE YOU LOVE HER.

It's just that life is a big ugly awkward cruel bitch.

And you surrender.

And stop trying to make a baby.

And start trying to find a baby.

And that leads you to a mammoth adventure . . .

Oh boy, though, do I understand the ache of that longing. It consumes you.

The interesting thing about the adoption process is that the social worker urges you to explore whether you feel you have grieved your infertility sufficiently. In other words, have you accepted it and said a proper goodbye to the child you will never have? I'm not sure exactly when I felt this had definitely happened, but the moment my little baby daughter was placed in my arms, any remnant of that longing became vapour and disappeared.

All there was, was her. Beautiful, bonny brown her.

Then, bam, it hit me. The awesome responsibility of her. A foot-long wriggling baby was going to be my biggest-ever commitment. Everything I thought mattered most until then just paled in comparison. I was her MOTHER for God's sake!

I am the one she will always rely on.

I am her protector and her advocate.

I am her role model for her own future motherhood, should she choose it.

I am called 'Mum'. Awesome.

I very quickly understood various things that became crashing realities and still are. Things like:

I can't always get it right. My own mum used to say, 'We don't do perfect', and it really helped. I was constantly doubting if I handled things correctly or if I said the right thing at the right moment. I know I often didn't, and it helps to know that it's OK.

I ALWAYS LOVE HER even if sometimes I don't like her choices or her behaviour. It's a God-given love and I am so grateful for it; it's seen us through some challenging moments.

She isn't me. Not in the slightest. It's nothing to do with biology, it's to do with the somewhat arrogant expectation that a kid will want to be a bit like you, want to emulate the family and how it works. Of course, they WON'T necessarily. This doesn't rule out the fact that she will no doubt enjoy family jokes or habits, but she will need to forge her own personality and that means straying from the furrow already ploughed. She seems to be a strange stranger to me, sometimes, but it's OK.

NEVER EVER will I attempt to be her 'friend'. I am not, and never will be and that's right. She can make and reject as many friends good and bad as she likes, but a mother needs to parent you, guide you and love you, not befriend you.

Step back and let mistakes happen, without helicoptering in to rescue all the time. I am still learning this and it might well be my hardest lesson. The fear is that I will misjudge it and the difficult 'tough love' will feel like neglect or the wrong choice. This is an area I have had to learn bravery in, and one thing I know for sure is that I would love to raise a brave kid, so I absolutely have to be just that.

The way we speak to kids becomes their inner voice. I read this somewhere, I can't remember where now, and I just know it's true. Be mindful of how you talk to and with them, they are set to record. I have heard myself coming out of her mouth on numerous occasions and it's fairly sobering!

Nothing is how I thought it would be. Actually, I'm not even sure I consciously thought much about how it would be, but I have somehow imagined an idea of parenting that comes from every representation I've seen on TV or film or in print. Why on earth I've been such a sucker, and bought all that aspirational crap, I don't know. Especially when my own actual experience of being a kid, mixed with everything I witness in all the real families around me, is tons more accurate and far preferable. Duh. Why, oh why, when I became a mother, did I think that a great childhood could only happen for my kid if the following ingredients were in plenteous evidence?:

- home-made cupcakes
- professional-quality face-painting
- flowery wellingtons
- festivals
- teepees
- angel/fairy wings
- Cath Kidston everything
- glamping
- babyccinos
- fairy lights
- beds in shape of a unicorn
- hats that make you look like a frog/raccoon
- trainers that put on own light show
- learn baby Mandarin educational toy
- baby gym membership

I'm sure all of the above are perfectly lovely, but I have to shake myself and remember that the following work just fine too:

- warm coat
- park
- crisps
- beach
- baked beans
- books
- Curly Wurlys
- skipping rope

I never felt authentic trying to emulate a Boden catalogue. It's gorgeous, but in truth I don't really know how to do it, so I gave up trying and instead did whatever came next that looked like good fun, and that was a blessed relief. Don't set yourself up to fail by trying to be someone else, it can NEVER work. Kids are the first to sniff out a disingenuous life. Make it real. It's not hard. In fact, it's miles easier than pretending.

Gilda Radner said that 'Motherhood is the biggest gamble in the world. It is the glorious life force. It's huge and scary – it's an act of infinite optimism.' When I find myself overwhelmed with the sheer size of the responsibility it often brings, those last words are the key. Optimism. That's right. I feel optimistic about the lives and the futures of my children, more so even than my own. I fear for the challenges they will face, some of which will be new to only their generation, but I have unquestionable faith in the actual people that they are, and I trust in their ability to face those challenges. So in them, all my optimism lives.

When I say 'them', I mean I have more than one child these days, because I am a stepmum, and it's honestly one of the biggest miracles of my life.

When I say 'child', they are of course adults really, but aren't your kids always children somehow?

I suppose I could refer to them as my stepson and stepdaughter, but there's something about the 'step' part that implies that I am a step away from caring as much. Of course I recognize and respect that I am not their blood mother. I wasn't there during their tiny years, I'm not part of the mesh of their family history, but I'm here now, and I ain't goin' anywhere. I have never met two people that I so easily, so instantly could love. The very first thing I noted about both of them was that, however much they thought they were covering it up, I knew, from the very first moment, that they were checking out if I was a good enough option for their dad, because they adore him and couldn't bear for him to be hurt.

She checked out if I was kind enough.

He checked out if I was funny enough.

Together they manned the drawbridge at the entrance of his heart and, however polite or gentle, I knew that none should pass unless they passed muster. Once through that test, once accepted as sufficient or better, the generosity with which they welcomed me and my girl in was heart-stopping. We very quickly realized that we were all meant to be together forever, and even though he and I hadn't moved on to the next level yet – we were still in 'dating' mode – the kids, all three, started to petition fairly publicly for nuptials. It would have been bum-clenchingly embarrassing if it wasn't so fabulously inevitable. All of a sudden, I had two new fully cooked kids in my life. Two humans full to the brim with ready-made personalities and acres of hopes and dreams.

What happened next, and has been ongoing for the last five years really, is . . . trust. Simple as that. Simple, yet ASTOUNDING when you consider that trust might be the last thing two different families who have been through two different divorces might be able to do.

It wasn't just me 'n' him getting married.

It was me 'n' my girl marrying him 'n' his girl and boy.

ALL of us got married, and as we stood there in the Cornish sea air and made our promises in front of all our beloveds, we wrapped that commitment around them all. In it together, bruises 'n' all. Betrothed.

All three of my kids have come to me in an interesting way, adopted or inherited. When Good Granny was alive, she commented to me that my daughter might not have come via my actual body, but that she definitely came via my heart. It's sentimental but true. Then later, two more arrived by the same route, and the love I feel for all three is visceral. Animal, almost. I would fight for them, I would lay my life down, I would have to, they ARE my life.

It's true to say that if you are properly connected, you are only ever as happy as your LEAST happy kid. I know this from personal experience. I have spent many hours over-thinking and over-feeling what's happening in their lives. I have no idea how to not do this . . . but I'm going to try and learn in this lifetime. I don't want to know how to disconnect from them, just how to disconnect from the worry. It seeps into every moment. But then, remember, 'we don't do perfect'. Thanks, Mum.

So, as a mum, is there anything I would hope to pass on to them? Of course I would love to gift my immense knowledge of all things in nature . . . names of trees and hedgerow flora and stuff, but the truth is I don't know any of that. That's big stuff. I only know small stuff, and so that is what I will pass on with pride. Stuff like:

- every day, clean slate
- be kind
- don't be late, value other people's time
- know what you can afford
- don't let anyone tell you you can't sing
- don't mix grape and grain
- dancing is a mood-shifter, do it every day, especially in lifts
- always poke fun at powerful people
- listen
- failure is useful
- you don't have to set fire to yourself to keep someone else warm
- don't contaminate chocolate with fruit
- take time for a decent poo
- be generous
- chew properly
- wrap up warm
- smile

I'd be blummin' delighted if any of that stuck. Sometimes I think we might be so busy trying to be great mothers that we forget it's the moments we don't notice or see, that THEY do. Those are the little Lego life blocks that go to build their childhoods, so that's really what we pass on, without even realizing it.

As Mother's Day approaches, and I will spend it without mine, I know where the valuable memories are, and I know how they sustain me. I know, for instance, that the pots I will use to cook lunch were hers, as were the rolling pin, the big wooden spoon and the water jug. I use them pretty much every day, just like she did, and when I get them out of the cupboard my childhood comes with them. My safe, happy childhood where my big-hearted mum cooked for us and where I never once doubted how loved I was . . . I am.

I know some people fear turning into their mothers. I certainly see her creeping further forward on to my face every single day in the mirror, but, y'know what? I LOVED her face. It's more than welcome on mine. She was here first, she was strong, and self-respecting. I should be so lucky to be a living reminder of her.

Make way for the mighty mothers!

MARCH

monday »

tuesday »

wednesday »

thursday »

friday »

saturday »

sunday »

MARCH

monday » ....

tuesday » ....

wednesday » ....

thursday » ....

friday »

saturday »

sunday »

MARCH

monday »

tuesday »

wednesday »

thursday »

friday »

saturday »

sunday »

MARCH

monday »

tuesday »

wednesday »

thursday »

friday »

saturday »

sunday »

MARCH

monday » ....

....

....

....

' ....

••

tuesday » ....

....

....

....

....

••

wednesday » ....

....

....

....

....

••

thursday » ....

....

....

....

....

••

friday »

saturday »

sunday »

April Fools

A few of the people who have made me laugh the most.

1. **Morecambe and Wise** – My whole family weak with laughter.

2. **Victoria Wood** – Goose fat and swimming hat.

3. **Jennifer Saunders** – Resting on my laurels.

4. **Elsie and Doris Waters** – The trailblazers.

5. **Sarah Silverman** – Want as BF.

6. **Lucille Ball** – Lips and pies.

7. **Laurel and Hardy** – One silly, one funny.

8. **Richard Pryor** – Because of everything.

9. **Robin Williams** – Because he was Robin Williams.

10. **Jessica Hynes** – Have slept with her so have to include her.

Your list starts here.

1. **French and Saunders** (this is non-negotiable).

2. _____

3. _____

4. _____

5. _____

6. _____

7. _____

8. _____

9. _____

10. _____

APRIL

Behold! Daffodils and tulips and all the bright confident light of April. Behold the Beauty.

Joan Collins said, 'The problem with Beauty is that it's like being born rich and getting poorer.'

I guess that's true if you're only thinking of Beauty as something on the outside of your body. And only if you regard getting older and the experience of physical change as solely deterioration. I know that scientifically we are all ageing from the moment we're born, but when it comes to Beauty, we make tons of stops along the way, and some of them are surprising.

Of course, physical Beauty is key, it'd be preposterous to deny it. The first minute we lay eyes on a person, we make all kinds of suppositions based on an endless feed of responses to superficial questions. Are they attractive? Are they fashionable? What is their skin/hair/teeth like? How tall/short/fat/thin are they? And on and on...

I so wish our first impressions could be concluded by asking much better questions like: Is this a substantial person? Can they look me in the eye? Do I instinctively believe they are honest/kind/funny? What's unique about the way they look? Do I trust them? What's lovely about them? Or intriguing?

I am as guilty as the next person of the superficial nonsense. Aesthetics are important. I know that. I know it matters that we are truthful about what we like when we look. BUT. Doesn't it also matter HOW we see? I can't bear that I have so clearly and so easily been manipulated into operating in such a narrow-minded way. The real sin of this brand of shallow, dabbly, instant judgement is that you can so easily overlook the tippest-toppest of most excellent people. I very nearly did that myself ...

I was writing my second novel, *Oh Dear Silvia*, which had a character in it who was a cocaine addict. I realized that my knowledge was massively restricted, so I did what you do when your mum used to run a rehab before she retired, and I called her to see how I could do some proper research. She recommended that I talk to the chap who took over from her as CEO when she retired – maybe he could help? Oh yes, him. Her colleague, who I'd met many, many times over the years. Tall bloke, silver hair, soft accent … him. I called him and he offered to try and set up a meeting between me and a couple of folk who use the facility he runs. I was dead impressed by the fact that, of course, his concern was more for the well-being, safety and confidentiality of those people. My research needs were way down his list of priorities. On the appointed day, I turned up and there he was on the step, ostensibly to greet me, but really, he was guarding everything and everyone inside. As he does.

I followed him up the stairs to his office. He had set the room up in such a way that, annoyingly, the two people I was due to interview were sitting with the only window at their backs, rendering them virtual silhouettes. It didn't really matter, I could see them well enough. They both spoke openly, generously, for over an hour, answering all my questions and giving me tons of helpful information regarding my story, and I knew by the end of my time with them that I had an authentic character, and that what I was intending to write about her was grounded in truth. This was a massive relief and when it was over and they were gone, I was happy to grab a quick cuppa with him in that same office and chew the cud a bit, but I was on a strict writing schedule, so didn't have much time for yap.

He sat down where they had been, so once again, in shadow against the light of the window behind him. I asked polite questions about his life, filling time really. I knew from his long-standing friendship with my mum that he was divorced and that he had two kids, so I asked after them. At which point he lit up, animated and clearly delighted to talk about them, the two most important people in his life. As he spoke, happily, proudly burbling on, a curious thing happened. The sun burst out from behind a cloud, and the lovely light poured in through the window, bounced off the white wall behind me and reflected, bam!, straight back onto his face, lighting him up as if Caravaggio and Fellini had collaborated. His gorgeous face was suddenly awash with beautiful bright light and for the first time ever, I SAW him. Really saw him. Beheld him. I stopped breathing for a moment while I took in his sea-blue eyes and the happy laughter lines around his mouth and the strong angle of his jaw. Then I noticed the width and strength of his shoulders and the muscle in his neck and how expressive his hands are... I knew in that instant that we would marry, yet a minute before, he was just that bloke who was a workmate of Mum's, nothing else. How on earth did I miss the beauty of him before, when I now think it's patently obvious? Remarkable, in fact.

Of course my mum later told me that this was the glorious work of my dead dad, ensuring from his place in heaven that I properly noticed what was right under my nose. Yeah, I know ... ridiculous ...

It's all about the beholder, isn't it? Perhaps we should consciously do much more beholding. 'Behold the sunrise', 'behold the egg and chips I just cooked you', 'behold your lovely legs which you appear to hate ...' Maybe if we did more beholding, it would remind us to find the Beauty, to look for it, rather than be told where to find it by magazines or the tellybox.

I saw a wonderful story recently, where some little kids in America used their mum's phone to surreptitiously take a picture of her fast asleep in her swimsuit on a beach. When she first saw it, she was horrified at the 'hideous big fat blob'. She was about to delete it when her son and daughter walked in, and she asked them if they knew anything about the dreadful picture. They admitted that they took it because they thought she 'looked so beautiful laying there', and 'it could be a postcard'. The kids loved the picture, and only saw their mum through adoring eyes, of course. The love was what made her beautiful to them. They beheld her. The Beauty really was in their eyes.

I know for sure that if someone I love is taking a picture of me, I look better. Beholding someone you love changes your face, your whole demeanour, so of course it would show. Photos are the perfect moment, captured in time, where you are responding to the photographer, when you are caught loving them. You can't tell me that isn't ALWAYS beautiful, because it is.

It's quite another thing to discuss Beauty directly with someone. I once sat next to an older woman in a theatre. A stranger. I was compelled to tell her in the interval that I thought she was the most beautiful person there. I knew I was crossing a boundary to do it, I knew I risked offending her, but I couldn't help it, it was true and I wanted her to know. Her beauty wasn't typical. There was something extraordinary about the way she held herself, her grace, her presence. Once I had summoned the courage to quietly tell her, I also noticed when she stood up that she had a magnificent bust to boot, and I've always been a huge fan of an unapologetic bosom. We spent the second act of the play next to each other in the darkness, and I was aware that I had most probably made her feel awkward, and I regretted that.

At the end of the play, she leaned over and thanked me for giving her 'just the tonic' she needed at 'a difficult time', called me 'cheeky' and off she went, rendered even more beautiful than before in my eyes by sheer dint of her self-effacing honesty. A brief and strange moment for both of us. Unforgettable.

It's a difficult thing to accept a compliment about your physical self. We are British and vanity is a sin. If acceptance comes too quickly, it's arrogance. Too much deflection is insincere. It's a minefield of possible social faux pas. We also doubt whether we are being told anything for real. Is it a trick? It can't be true, so why is this person saying it? What do they want from me? We are innately suspicious.

I have huge misgivings about any compliments made about my physical self. I can't accept a compliment for something I didn't create or achieve, surely? Maybe it would be more palatable if we complimented each other with 'nice DNA' . . .?

As for the rest of my body, my relationship with it, my fluctuating weight, my determination to remain friends with my shape whatever size it is, all of this and the relentless scrutiny of it through the press, have taught me to keep tight-lipped, because almost anything I do say on this subject is misconstrued or misquoted. I do not set out to be anyone's role model or anyone's soundbite or anyone's example. However, if by simply doing my job without any body shame, I am an example of someone just pegging on, then so be it. If a plump girl writing funny stories in a notebook in her bedroom thinks, well it didn't stop Dawn French . . . then, great. All of that is by the by. The more challenging times are moments of clarity I have when well-meaning interviewers say something like 'you're looking so well', when I instinctively feel that what they're really saying is 'you're not as fat any more'. And that is true. I'm not. But I'm not any better than when I was fatter. Perhaps I'm healthier, and that's what they really mean, in which case, say that. I don't want to be tricked into believing that the old, heavier me was somehow less valuable or attractive, because that's simply not my truth, and neither is it the truth of so many bigger women.

On the other hand, it's tempting to argue that it's churlish to be irritated by a compliment, that I should be so lucky, and that I should show grace in accepting. It's true of course that if we present to the world in an agreeable way, our passage through life is inestimably easier. That agreeable, acceptable way though, is narrowly defined and hugely manipulated, and I suppose that's the bit I am irritated by, on behalf of myself and plenty of other fabulously flawed women. If we were looking to behold the beauty in each other in lots of different ways, we surely wouldn't feel we had to conform?

I was once utterly overwhelmed by Beauty to the point of sobbing. I was on holiday with my then husband and my best friend and her chap, in Barcelona. Like all visitors to that fantastic city, we visited various Gaudí buildings and parks. The last one we went to was the Güell Palace, a huge, splendid, privately commissioned townhouse built in 1886. All Gaudí buildings take your breath away, they just do, there is simply no other architect like him. From the outside, the building is austere, huge and grey, with lots of twiddly ironwork. Inside though, is even more astonishing. We went up various staircases and saw beautiful marble balustrades and vast religious portraits and fabulous wooden parquet floors, until finally we entered the central hall which is the height of at least two floors and has wonderful long windows with stained glass and a high cupola. I couldn't speak, it was so supremely beautiful. We moved on up through to a first-floor salon where the tall art nouveau windows have stone arches in front of them. Parabolic arches, which as I understand it, is the shape a ball makes if you throw it in the air, a high arch, lofty, organic and elegant. The shape is very pleasing. By this time, I was tingling inside, a curious excitement I couldn't entirely understand. The next part of the building was a corridor with the same exquisite arches. Half-way along, I started to cry inexplicably. I immediately wanted to get into some fresh air to take stock of what was happening inside me, it was strange and powerful. I split off from the group and headed up some stairs to the roof and stepped out into the nippy air, only to find myself in a surreal roof garden of eccentric, oddly shaped chimney stacks covered with colourful mosaics of broken Arabic tiles. A weird whimsy, an inner-city forest of ceramic trees, so different to the gravely handsome building beneath. I had come up to recover from the heady effect the building was having on me, only to find even more delights. They tipped me into a sensory overload. I started to sob, and I couldn't stop. I had to sit down and surrender to it. Something about the dynamic, elemental architecture of the building had chimed with me in a kind of perfect rhythm. A heartbeat rhythm. We had the same pulse, somehow. I felt that I already knew that building, that I completely understood it. Perhaps the simple fact is that the potent Beauty of it all, made me LONG to be in sync with it. I wanted to belong there. I have not experienced the brute force of that Beauty punch in the gut in any other building before or since. It took me a few days and several Riojas to come down from that sublime high. I haven't been back. I don't think I want to, in case it doesn't happen again.

I want to get my Beauty fixes in everyday, manageable bite-size chunks so they don't capsize me. For instance, I will ALWAYS find Beauty in the sight of:

- the perfect flick at the edge of my daughter's eyeline
- Bodmin Moor from the A30
- my new dog's spotty belly
- mackerel flicking about in the sea
- my husband's collection of sea glass
- correctly stacked cream tea. (Jam then cream, please. Always.)
- the big, big Cornish sky
- my father-in-law's wink

All of these I can have buckets of, anytime I like, and that will do.

APRIL

monday »

tuesday »

wednesday »

thursday »

friday »

saturday »

sunday »

APRIL

monday »

tuesday »

wednesday »

thursday »

friday »

saturday »

sunday »

APRIL

monday »

tuesday »

wednesday »

thursday »

friday »

saturday »

sunday »

APRIL

monday »

tuesday »

wednesday »

thursday »

friday »

saturday »

A WEDDING WEEKEND
BY THE SEASHORE
19th-21st April 2013

sunday »

APRIL

monday »

tuesday »

wednesday »

thursday »

friday »

saturday »

sunday »

I Instantly Smile When:

1. Little kids fall over (I know it's wrong, but . . .).

2. Eddie Izzard tells stories.

3. I hear that voicemail which starts, 'So sorry, but we aren't going to be able to make it to yours . . .'

4. Husband tells me he wants to open a sweet shop.

5. The waitress says, 'I'm sorry, but we only have white bread . . .'

6. Mother-in-law invites us over for pasty night.

7. I see dog every morning.

8. Cat hides in my clothes.

9. ANY baby is nearby . . . It's embarrassing.

Your list starts here.

1. _____

2. _____

3. _____

4. _____

5. _____

6. _____

7. _____

8. _____

9. _____

10. _____

MAY

I have a little treasure to offer you.

It's the most simple, easy, obvious thing, but it's somehow kept as a mystery.

It can change your life for the better.

It CAN'T change it for the worse.

It's a little box. Open it. Inside are two words written on a piece of paper.

STILL and SILENT.

In those two words, there is real magic.

Believe me.

I know.

Now then, I have to confess that I am that person who, if you say the word 'mindfulness', might make a sucky-lemon face, so cynical am I. My friend Ruby Wax, who writes so well about all that, has changed my thinking. A bit. But on the whole, I can't be doing with prescriptive quasi-Buddhist new-age lessons-in-life stuff. I know proper mindfulness isn't that, but still. I love a bit of wisdom or advice or the odd metaphor, oh yes I do, but moving 'towards the light' is dangerous ground for me. If I find it absurd, I find it funny and thus utterly dispensable, that's the problem. It's a curse sometimes, because my desire to enjoy the laugh is greater than my desire to find the deeper meaning, however much the latter might be tons better for me. I do want to learn new profound things but I don't want to learn them from an ocean-going wanker. Sorry to be strict about this, but life is too interesting to have my focus pulled away from it by some airy fairy long-winded esoteric twot. Say something original and I am yours, I will respect you forever. I will wash your car, I will wash your feet, I will wash your mother. Waste my precious time with twaddle and I will put you closer to your God, I swear it.

Mindful? My mind is already full, thank you. Full of vet appointments, work deadlines and fantasy pasty fillings. Why would I want it to be even fuller?

I know, I know, but . . . you know what I mean? I haven't got the TIME to be mindful, I'm bleddy busy, like all of us.

And anyway, I like my mind being busy – being busy is living. All of the appointments that fill up this VERY diary mean so many things to me:

I am loved.

I am loving someone.

I am loving lots of someones.

I am working.

I am looking after my teeth.

I am remembering.

I am needed.

I don't want to stop being busy. Busy is rather beautiful and being told to be otherwise is yet another of those unachievable goals that leave me feeling hopeless, like being a Kardashian or spiralizing, or vajazzling. We are all busy. Let's NOT stop. It's great!

YES, YES, YES, to all that.

BUT . . .

Here's the thing. I am not advocating that we remove the busy clutter of our lives. That's my energy, my purpose, I just don't want to be OVERWHELMED by it, that's all. I want to notice it, I don't want to miss anything simply because my diary's too full, and my head's too frenetic.

I know something very key about myself which is this: the small stuff is my favourite stuff, but it's the first stuff to drop off the edge of a busy life unless you pay attention. I want to sit up and be alert so's I register and enjoy all that lovely small stuff.

Recently, an older woman I admire a lot told a story in my earshot. It went like this: she was a young girl when her father taught her how to row a boat. They rowed together in the river and he showed her how to use the oars. The time came for her to row the boat on her own. He stayed on the shore and she tentatively rowed out into the middle of the river. She was doing OK until quite suddenly the weather changed. The wind picked up, dark storm clouds came in and pelted the little boat with rods of rain. She was very scared on the choppy river, and shouted to her father to tell him so. From the shore, and over the din of the storm, she hears his voice booming out, instructing her to 'Sit still, hold tight, look up!' She followed this advice, calmed down and eventually rowed back to the safety of the shore and her father's arms. She explained that these three simple instructions became a sort of mantra she has carried with her ever since, and she has found them hugely useful to remember, especially if you're in a pickle.

Sit still.
Hold tight.
Look up.

It's exactly what I need to remember to do. It helps me to be steady.

I heard that story around the time that I decided to start a new habit, and on reflection, they are connected. I love that kind of congruence, when a couple of seemingly random things float together in a perfect timely fusion.

A habit sounds like a bad thing. This isn't. It's a wonderful thing, and it started one May morning when I was out walking my old (now, sadly, dead) dog, Dolly. We walked up the familiar hill near our home, through a narrow lane with overhanging trees bordered by stone walls with primroses poking through. On one side of the track there is a steep bank with a row of houses above. On the opposite side is a deep, wooded valley. There are various breaks in the wall where you can escape the well-trodden path and dart into the woods. I have often done this and I have enjoyed the fact that I am near enough to the track to hear the passers-by. Sometimes, if their frequency is right, I can hear EVERY WORD they say! I know you shouldn't eavesdrop ... yeah ... but I do, and I like it.

Anyway, on this one occasion, I was in the valley, clambering over a huge fallen tree trunk, and there was a fabulous shagpile of bluebells all around. The sunlight was flickering through the tall beech trees and dancing mischievously on the cobalt flowers and it was breathtaking. I was overcome with a sudden desire to lie down, so I did. Dolly was a bit confused; this was highly unusual, but she was ancient and tired so didn't resist. There was a nip in the May morning air, but it was dry so I lowered myself on to the crunchy forest floor, trying not to crush any precious plants, and I lay still, right next to the big thick tree, my dog breathing steadily by my side and I looked up.

Up.

Up through the leafy canopy to where I could see chunks of blue sky beyond. I rarely see this sight and it was gorgeous, surreal. Why had I not done this every single day, such a simple achievable instant hit of natural beauty, right on my doorstep? Never mind the phenomenal eye Beauty, the ear Beauty, nose Beauty, fingertips Beauty and ultimately the heart Beauty were ALL tickled awake. As my quickened-from-fast-walking heartbeat slowly slowed down, along with my breath, so my spirits rose, and a sublime calm flooded into me. My body, mind and heart were all ticking at exactly the same rhythm. Then my breathing deepened, and I felt like I was sinking backwards, downwards into the bracken underneath me. Sinking yet supported, I just surrendered to the vast perfect peace of it all. The stillness was the loveliest part. 'True silence is to the spirit what sleep is to the body — nourishment and refreshment' - W.Penn. To be still, silent and awake rather than asleep was a revelation.

I loved

loved

loved it.

And now it's my 'habit' and I try to do it as often as possible, sneak into private places, lie down, look up, and find some minutes to travel inwards a bit, give my head time to hear my own quiet inner voice, normally so muted by loud living. That's when I remember things I've forgotten, and when I allow distant nagging suspicions to be heard. My best creative and instinctive thinking happens then, when it's just me and nature, and silence. Not a single second of the silences I've known has been a waste of my time. It's been the BEST use, because in those stillnesses I have allowed myself to plumb and dredge some hope and optimism up from the sediment of deep fundamental places I don't ordinarily visit. I am truthful in these moments. As truthful as I can bear.

'You are never more essentially yourself,
than when you are still'
Eckhart Tolle

There's no doubt that if you can find a few minutes to leave space where words usually live, thoughts can come and inhabit that same place. Of course, it's not always totally silent. Our world isn't.

But I am silent. So then not only can I think, but I can also listen. And not not not talk.

Oh, it's such a fantastic rest.

And it's such a release to let my heart unpeel, and to sit quietly with my sadnesses and my joys, uninterrupted by the loud squawking need for instant reactivity. I don't know about you, but I am always feeling the need to react immediately to everything. We are all so impatient, my blood boils over the tiniest little wait. I have forgotten somehow that I am utterly entitled to some peace and calm because without it, I will boil over.

The absolute best thing about lying down and looking up is that if you can gently moderate your breathing and clear your mind of silly insistent petty stuff, those terrier thoughts that constantly nip at your brain, you can view the real world from the underneath, so to speak. As if you're at the bottom of the ocean where, even if there's a ferocious storm up above, all is muted and calm on the sea bed.

Now, don't mistake this quiet for air and light and froth only. Silence is potent and can be muscular. I have found strength in silent moments to sit down hard on any angers or hatreds or jealousies. I have confronted some demons there and I have managed to process my difficult stuff through the filters of the silence. It really is powerful, and I can't be without it, because, the truth is, my inner compass is only activated when I give it the time and the quiet. It's a delicate mechanism that can't work well when jolted about.

Of course, the true balance happens when there is a lovely noisy life as well as a lovely quiet life. Some of the noise is utter joy, like when your kids laugh till they fart, or when you're ALL singing along to Adele in the car, or when someone is frothing milk for your coffee, or when THAT person's footfall is on your stairs.

Noise is good.

Silence is gooder.

That's all.

MAY

monday »

tuesday »

wednesday »

thursday »

friday »

saturday »

sunday »

MAY

monday »

tuesday »

wednesday »

thursday »

friday »

saturday »

sunday »

MAY

monday »

tuesday »

wednesday »

thursday »

friday »

saturday »

sunday »

MAY

monday »

tuesday »

wednesday »

thursday »

friday »

saturday »

sunday »

MAY

monday »

tuesday »

wednesday »

thursday »

friday »

saturday »

sunday »

THAT Letter....

On the next page is the chance to write THAT letter. The one you've been meaning to write. You know the one, and you know who it's to. If you're struggling, it might start with one of the following ...

- I'm so sorry about ...

- I want to say thank you for ...

- I really want to know what happened ...

- I really want to tell you what happened ...

- I am writing to ask your forgiveness ...

- Please help me to understand ...

- I've always wanted to tell you ...

- I'm writing to ask you to return my ...

- I've been thinking ...

- This is the most difficult letter I've ever had to write ...

(When you're finished, you might cut it out, and keep it in the flap at the back of this book. For now.)

Dear

Advice To Be Ignored

DON'T pour in tea without the milk first or you get a ginger husband.

DON'T go out with wet hair.

DON'T swim within eight hours of eating.

DON'T keep your coat on indoors or you won't feel the benefit.

DON'T take sweets from strangers.

DON'T move without stretching first.

DON'T wake me up before you go go.

DON'T lick a cat's bottom.

Take a picture of yourself as you are right now,

and place it here.

SUMMER

The dog days of Summer.

What ARE they? Is it when dogs are so hot they collapse on the ground? Kind of.

Dog days. The sultry part of the Summer, supposed to occur during the period that Sirius, the Dog Star, rises at the same time as the sun: now often reckoned to be from July 3rd – August 11th. A period marked by lethargy, inactivity or indolence.

For me, Summer really begins in the last two weeks of June when the suddenly very green full-grown grass in fields is instantly mottled with tons of colour from all the wild flowers. Daisies and buttercups and poppies and forget-me-nots. Above these are the butterflies teasing the flowers and above these are the midges and mayflies showing off their impressive synchronized dance displays. Poor ol' mayflies, I wonder if they know they only live for a day or so? Maybe they do, and maybe that's why their dance is so very urgent. They are born, they grow, they mate, they dance, they die, all inside forty-eight hours. Quick little happy lives, which have been lived at this jolly speed for millions of years. Natural history tells us that mayflies flitted around the ears of dinosaurs, no doubt showing them the exact same moves they show us today. Short lives, long history.

There are bees and birds and blossom. There are strawberries and cream, and elderflower and clover and dragonflies and mackerel and blue skies and wispy clouds. And most of all, in those long hot days there is gladness.

The bald fact is that we don't survive without light. It warms our brittle British bones and feeds our skin some vital Vitamin D goodness. So, thank you, sun, for coming to visit us in the dog days, and try not to listen when we gripe on about how sweaty, sluggish and uncomfortable we are. That's how we show our happy. The constant whinge is our version of gratitude.

Summer feels like totally the present to me. The absolute now, in a way that other seasons don't. Perhaps it's because our remembrance of the endless summers of childhood is so delightful that we constantly want to summon it. When Summer comes around we imbue it with memories of long days when time stood still and tea time was a week away. Did being smaller make time seem bigger? It was huge and soft and forever and limitless.

Did I ever give a moment's thought then to being 'beach body ready'? No, thank God. I had my body and I was ready to take it to the beach. I didn't give a monkey's about how it would be regarded by anyone else. I had no idea what shame or embarrassment were. Or waxing or shaving or varnishing. I wanted the warm sand between my toes and to feel the bite of hot golden sun on my shoulders making lines where my straps were. I wanted to catch my breath as I ran into the icy Cornish water then squeal with pleasure as my flesh gradually became as cold. All of my energy went into defeating giant waves, punching them into submission. Occasionally, I would lose and be dragged under and tumbled around inside a cleverer wave than me, reminding me who was ultimately in charge. A couple of times, I genuinely wondered if I would get out, get up, get through, and when I eventually emerged gasping and spluttering and nearly dead, I pretended I'd done it on purpose and that it was thrilling. No way would I ever let my brother know I had almost drowned. Now, THAT would constitute real shame.

I remember being so tired after long beach days full of fresh air and salt that I fell asleep with my forehead in my spaghetti hoops, and couldn't have been happier.

It's that essential warmth and easy responsibility-free contentment that we try repeatedly to recapture as we grow up. We long for one more snatch of it.

The Summer of our lives is for me the ages twenty-five to fifty years. The growing-up years. You can no longer claim youth as your excuse for making mistakes, you have to own the fact that you might just be an idiot sometimes.

As I write, my own two daughters are twenty-five. Their twenty-five seems completely different to my memory of mine, but I guess every generation says the same thing. Why are we given to believing that we somehow had it harder? We didn't. We had it different. I think that probably my life was slower and considerably less cluttered or noisy. The constant pinging and yakking of phones and social media and online everything played no part in my twenties. I would have been the first to submit to it, I'm sure.

No, MY twenties were all about trying to be seriously in love. By seriously I mean that I was most definitely on the lookout for a permanent mate. I was done with the awkward and strange world of dating, I wanted someone to grow alongside.

```
'Someone to hold you too close

Someone to hurt you too deep

Someone to sit in your chair

And ruin your sleep

And make you aware of being alive.'
```

I was also in love with all things Stephen Sondheim, as you can see, and like all good FagHags, I desperately wished his lyrics applied to me. They didn't. They applied to dysfunctional middle-aged, sophisticated New Yorkers. I so wished I was that ...

In my twenties and thirties, I was someone fully immersed in the burgeoning eighties comedy scene in London, without even knowing that's what it was. A series of happy accidents took Fatty and me right into the heart of a buzzing movement: the 'alternative' circuit. Again, I was pretty much clueless that we were at the eye of that particular cultural storm. We were motivated mainly by lager, laughs and lust. I started to realize it was becoming de rigueur amongst the glitterati to turn up at the Comic Strip (which was then a strip joint in Soho) to watch our shows when the likes of Dustin Hoffman and Jack Nicholson and Robin Williams put in appearances. When Michael Palin later turned up, and came backstage to talk to us in the dressing room as if we were equals, it blew my tiny star-struck mind.

It was also at the Comic Strip that I met my first husband, who came to watch one night. Jennifer met Ade there too, although it would be a while before they officially got together. All of us at the Comic Strip were pretty much the same age, and when Jennifer and I joined the line-up, very few of us had any real responsibilities. We could fly off to Australia for the Adelaide Festival, we could move to Hope Cove in Devon for eight weeks of filming or we could take the first available cheap flight to anywhere (Malta in the end) to write. Utter freedom.

When you are devoid of responsibilities in this way, of course, you don't even know it. Good in a way, because that in itself would be a responsibility. For me though, a person who takes my commitments and obligations very seriously, too seriously, it might have been handy to have known at the time just how halcyon those days were. Those lighter days when the biggest dilemma was whether you would have enough dosh to pay your next rent, and the worst thing that would happen even then, would be that you had to sleep on a mate's sofa for a couple of weeks, and that in itself was a laugh, so … not that bad really. When all you owned were two suitcases of clothes and shoes and a couple of embarrassing soft toys brought from your childhood bedroom under the premise of being 'lucky' or 'a collection'. Oh and a few albums including Lionel Bart's *Oliver!* and the hits of Herb Alpert nicked from the parents' collection. The most prized and therefore most scratched album was of course *Tapestry* by Carole King. I was convinced every song was my signature tune. How did she know me so well?! How did she know that I wanted so much to 'feel like a natural woman'? And, incidentally ... how DOES that feel?

I went from flat-sharing and all the concomitant joys and horrors of that, to . . .

Actually, excuse me a moment, just want to fact-check those memories . . .

FLAT-SHARING IN MY TWENTIES

Joys	Horrors
larks with Jennifer	mouldy quiche
toga parties	mouldy soup
being democratic	other people's hair
	other people's boyfriends
	other people's sex noises
	cleaning rota
	ghosts
	constant door slams
	other people's feet
	waiting cross-legged for fuggy bathroom
	other people's music
	divvying up bills
	arguments about smoking
	mess
	other people
	being democratic

Oh yeah, it was QUITE good fun. SOMETIMES.

Once, when I shared a house with Fatty and several others, we had a break-in and the police came to look round. We waited downstairs while they hunted about for evidence. When they came to talk to us, they said that all was pretty much in order except obvious stuff that was missing like the telly, etc., but they were particularly dismayed by the awful state the thieves had left the attic bedroom in – a disgusting mess of emptied-out drawers and dirty laundry all over the place, uncalled for and disrespectful. Abusive. We didn't tell them that was the only room the burglars HADN'T disturbed. That was Jennifer's room, pretty much as it always was . . .

I hasten to add that she is no longer the chaos monkey she was back then. Quite the opposite in fact. Somewhere in her thirties, she discovered power hoses and her messy world became a cleaner, more ordered one almost overnight. She was different then. As was I.

When I say 'different', do I mean simply 'younger'? She is still essentially the person I met when I was nineteen, and so am I, but now we're both miles further down the road of working out who we truly are. I don't think I made many decisions in my twenties and thirties that had a grown-up, proper authentic me at the helm. Everything I decided to do came from a fairly narrow set of options that, back then, I considered to be a huge world-is-my-oyster of choices. I basically chose between the A or B that was on offer. I was fortunate that those As and Bs were fairly exciting, and led me to some interesting places, but when I reflect on those years now, I wasn't truly navigating, I was attempting to steer as best I could in a fast-flowing river, which was taking me wherever IT was going.

Big, huge decisions sort of made themselves and then I lived them. Decisions like who to marry and what job to do and whether to make a family of our own and where to live and who to take care of all kind of tumbled down the slippy banks into my youthful river, and swept me along.

At twenty-five I was still a kid at heart, but with independence and a bit of dosh and the seeds of a future career. I didn't really give a monkey's about any of it because there were lager and laughs and lust and the sun was shining and I was twenty-five.

By the time I was thirty, quite a lot had changed. I didn't pay rent any more. I paid a mortgage. I was a married person with someone else's well-being to put before mine, and a whole new family of in-laws to pay attention to. New people, with a different accent, background, colour to me. A big gang of people, ever lovin', ever-expandin', who welcomed me into a world of ackee and saltfish, curry goat and rice 'n' peas. (I later attempted my own version, rice 'n' pies, not so good).

I was suddenly a person who travelled for work, and I was involved in something called 'a company', which meant I had legal responsibilities, whatever they might be. I still didn't really take that much seriously because thirty is quite close to twenty-five, isn't it . . .? I was still practically twenty-five. . .

One night, I went to bed and when I woke up the next morning, I was forty. Literally, by the time I woke up. I'm not called Dawn for nuttin' . . . I was born right then, at dawn.

I had a young daughter, a busy husband, a crammed work-life and a giant millstone of a mortgage. Time seemed to have retreated under a rock, nowhere to be seen.

Lots of people helped me to get loads done . . .

Someone helped me by picking my kid up from school and making her tea until I could get home.

Someone helped me by changing our beds each week and keeping the house tidy.

Someone helped me by sorting out my diary and checking I was where I was supposed to be.

Someone helped me by sorting out all my work commitments and checking the deals.

Someone helped my to organize all my finances properly and pay the right taxes.

Someone helped me to keep a car on the road ... and on ... and on ...

Someone.

Someone.

Someone.

And somewhere along the fast-flowing river, ten years whizzed by and someone ... was present in my life but it was hardly me, I was always disappearing around the next bend, way way ahead.

Lucky me to have the first-world problem that is a happy, busy, well-supported life, I know, but still it wouldn't have hurt to stop for a minute and drink it all in. Now I'm left with a blur, and some photographs as evidence.

Something I really did learn about in this very creatively fertile part of my life was friendship. I lost a couple of beloveds to cancer, accidents and Aids, and I learnt that however fast or mindlessly I was living it, life is inestimable, and just living it isn't enough, I needed to ATTEND to it. I was on the front foot at all times, and as we know, any time spent on one foot is unstable time. I needed to plant both feet on the floor every now and again, so that I could feel exactly that – surefooted.

It was ALWAYS friends who reminded me of this, my closest inner circle of trusted darlins, the ones I could hear anything from, however difficult. Likewise, it was in this period of my life that I started a quiet, subtle cull.

Don't worry, I didn't murder anyone. Though . . . I was sorely tempted on occasion, believe me.

Turning forty served to remind me that time marches on, and when I organized my fortieth birthday party, I had the very sobering experience of having to draw up the list of guests for the party. We were limited for space so I knew that some difficult choices had to be made. At the time, I considered cancelling the whole damn thing for fear of offending. Offending who? People I hadn't seen very much of? People I perhaps had drifted from? People I perhaps couldn't remain close to for various reasons? People who were bad for me? People I was bad for?

We all have these trying moments in our lives, usually in the form of weddings, anniversaries, christenings and birthdays. The high days and holidays. This is when we have to work out what we really feel about those around us. I HATED the seeming brutality of the choosing. It's far easier to bumble along happily in life not ever having to confront challenging social decisions, inviting everyone to everything, but then you can't ever have a moment where those gathered around you are ALL those you truly love and it's in these rare moments that real nourishment occurs. For everyone. It's also totally lovely to know that you are part of someone else's inner circle too; it's the ultimate acknowledgment of the love you share and the history of that, the gradual building it has taken for the foundations to be so solid.

My desire to have real conversations with my friends and family with a marked absence of hyperbole or flattery or cynicism became very strong. It must have been trying for them. It was as if I was pulling on my moorings, checking they were safe. I had no place for string, only sturdy rope. I needed resilient, industrial tensile-strength chums with enduring staying power. I worked out who they were in my forties and miraculously, they are still there today, wrapped around me, mooring me up forever. Thank you, God, or whoever, for all the right things they constantly say and do. And well done me for making heroically correct choices.

It has been these few noble mountaineers who have taught me the following:

- There is no need to be perfect, ever
- Someone else's achievements are not your failings
- Someone else's mistakes don't belong to you
- Every now and then, a bit of rejection does you good
- Don't resist pain, else it grows and becomes suffering, which is tons worse
- Trust your instincts
- Resist too much gambling/porn/fast food/drugs/booze/all-boy strip shows
- It's OK to say NO without having to explain
- The ideal antidote to frustration is gratitude
- It's possible to change your mind
- Never EVER be alone in a house without chocolate
- Nothing, nothing, nothing is more significant than love

My intense love for my daughter coloured all of my forties. There is something fantastically liberating about conceding to yourself that absolutely no-one will ever matter as much as this little chick. It was EASY to be devoted to her, she was hugely loveable and remarkable and I had longed for her. Of course, she was also lots of things I hadn't quite anticipated, like feisty and cheeky and naughty. And I was lots of things I hadn't anticipated, like impatient and tired and exasperated, which made for a heady mother–daughter mix on occasion, but whatever battles we fought, that lovely ol' rope was there, tying us up securely together at all times.

The ferocious strength of my feelings for her also had a price, which I think is quite common for parents, and that is a sudden and morbid fear of accident or death that might leave her abandoned. It's a ridiculous, misguided over-dramatic fear, I know that, but I was inordinately haunted by it for a good ten years. I couldn't bear to imagine my life without her or her life without me. If I allowed myself to dwell on it for too long, I could be reduced to a blubbering wreck with all my tortured imaginings. It was clearly a process I had to pass through because I hardly ever think like this now. Maybe that's because I have, at least, managed to grow her into her twenties, which is older than I was before I lost a parent, and I survived that, so I wonder if this is my measure?

In my forties she was still my baby, but totally not a baby at all any more. Everything and everyone was changing too quickly. Except me, of course. The mirror was telling me I was forty-something but inside my head, I was twenty-five.

I read articles that told me to dress appropriately for my age, to do Pilates and to take vitamins. Oh do eff off, please. You don't understand, I was twenty-five only ten minutes ago, this isn't the real me!

I have never actively resisted ageing, I have simply not quite believed it. I am not ashamed to tell my age to anyone, anytime, whoever wants to know. I am just astonished at how it comes about while you are not paying attention.

And look out ... while I was busy blethering on and looking the other way, here comes FIFTY!!!

For me? Whaaat?!?!

> 'I believe that everyone else my age
> is an adult whereas I am merely in disguise'
> Margaret Atwood

Good Questions to Ask
and Answer

- What's stopping you? _____

- What do you wish you could do more of? _____

- Which song do you know all the words to? _____

- Which song belongs to you? _____

- How are you? _____

- Who can you call in the middle of the night? _____

- Who do you wish was your new best friend? _____

- More like Mum or Dad? _____

- What do you picture when you think of happiness? _____

- What could you do better? _____

- What last made you actually laugh out loud? _____

- Most favourite meal ever? _____

- Best thing you can cook? _____

- Thing you're really good at? _____

- What do you neglect? _____

- What job would you do if money wasn't a consideration? _____

- Biggest crush? _____

- Which house would they put your blue plaque on? _____

- What did your parents get right? _____

- Do you have a philosophy? _____

- What scares you? _____

- Which memory makes you shudder? _____

- The best cake in the world? _____

- The cleverest person you know? _____

- Who do you wish was your mentor? _____

- The best thing that happened last year? _____

- When you got it most right? _____

- The worst fib you told? _____

- The compliment that mattered most? _____

- One thing you know for certain? _____

- Who would you want at your deathbed? _____

- What do you have faith in? _____

- Who do you have faith in? _____

JUNE

In this warm, cheerful month, I want to mainly say some thank yous, so here goes:

REASONS TO BE GRATEFUL (PART I)

THANK YOU, Mrs McKeown, the Head Teacher at Parliament Hill School for Girls way back in 1981. I was a young probationary teacher working in the drama department then. The head of drama wasn't in the best of health and although I was an 'inexperienced' newbie, there was a rare chance for me to be fast-tracked to a more senior position much sooner than I'd imagined. Teaching was my utter passion, there wasn't another job I wanted more . . . until Jennifer told me about the Comic Strip, a small group of alternative comedians looking for new acts (women in particular) to join the line-up. We auditioned, we joined, we worked six nights a week with me moonlighting from my day job. I was knackered but very happy. Then the day came when we were offered the chance to take the Comic Strip show to the Adelaide Festival in Australia. Everyone else was free to go except me. I had my proper job, with all the responsibilities that entailed, I couldn't just leave it in the middle of term. I agonized over the dilemma. In the end I decided to seek the advice of Mrs McK, the very person whose wrath I could incur, considering the fact that I shouldn't have had a second job at all!

Well, the twenty-minute meeting I had with her was a masterclass in selfless wisdom. She acknowledged the naughtiness, the dilemma and the circumstances, including her own need not to lose another member of staff in that department at such a key time. After considering it all, she told me that in life, you HAVE to take opportunities when they come, and that she would not forgive herself if she prevented me from going although that would've suited the school more. She gave me her blessing to go, and said there would be a job there for me on my return should I want it. I left her office in tears of gratitude. Had she been otherwise and demanded that I stick to my duty, I think I might still be there now, no bad thing, but ...y'know ...that Australian tour was the beginning of a whole new adventure, so, ta to the sagacious Mrs McK. I have always tried to remember that if people around me need to fly the nest for bigger, better or even just different jobs, it's best to let them go with grace.

THANK YOU **for being alive**. We've had a dodgy few years where our world has lost some giants. Far too many accidents and incidents. For a while it has felt as if there was another shocking loss every day, like the Earth was slightly off its axis and people were dropping away. I lost some friends and family too. It feels massively unfair and gut-wrenchingly sad. My very-clever-indeed uncle, the historian Dr Michael O'Brien, who was a mighty intellectual, suddenly had cancer and died far too quickly. Along with the rest of the family and especially his darlin' wife, we know that he is gone – we are just left wondering ...where?

THANK YOU, **Jimmy Moir**, the head of Entertainment at the BBC in the eighties, who sat Fatty and me down in his office, and explained that although he didn't personally get what was funny about *French and Saunders*, clearly enough other people did, so he was prepared to 'put my dick on the table', and give us our own series. And thank you to him also for not actually putting his dick on the table.

Although ...perhaps he did? And maybe I just couldn't see it ...?

THANK YOU to our fantastic country for two main reasons:

If you get sick, someone looks after you and you don't have to pay (a fact as I write. Not sure for how much longer . . .?)

There are NO deadly poisonous snakes or spiders.

There are hardly any earthquakes.

There are no man-eating sharks.

THANK YOU for me being past the menopause, which turned out to be a confusing jumble of a time where I didn't recognize any of my body or mind's behaviour. Thank you for me NOT murdering anyone in my immediate environs. Thank you for them not murdering ME, who, frankly, deserved it more.

THANK YOU to my parents, the greatest loves of my life, for teaching me such a lot of good stuff. Most of it was about self-belief, family and real love. The Frenchies often managed to get a lot of things just that little bit wrong, but the things we got right were truly the best of all things.

Although I lost my dad far too soon and too suddenly, I can definitely say that, thankfully, in the case of my mum, we were able, conversely, to say everything we wanted to before she died, quite quickly, at the age of seventy-seven. I am so grateful for that, because everyone deserves to hear, if it is true, that when their life is eventually weighed in the balance they are found to have been a superlative human and a wonderful parent, notwithstanding all the maddening, glorious flaws. She heard that from us. She knew it. Then she died. So that's OK by me. Yes. That'll do.

THANK YOU for work, for it being creative and enjoyable and challenging. Much as I find a lot that I do quite daunting, I have never once wished I didn't do it. I have always wanted to turn up. My mum used to tell me that 'showing off' was most unattractive. Oh yeah? Well, now it's my ruddy job! There were honestly times when I was making *French and Saunders* with Fatty back in the day, when there was very little difference to being ten years old in my bedroom, rifling about in the dressing-up box, making up silly characters and doing funny voices to make my friend laugh. How did this become an actual job?! Recently I've been feeling that because we spent so much time in front of the camera arsing about for so long, I am happy to retreat from so much of the showbizzy jazz-hands attention, and be at home being quiet and writing more. It doesn't mean that I don't want a bit of that plugged-in-to-an-audience type of buzz every now and then. That's why I took my one-woman show on tour for eighteen months, and that's why I agreed to host a kids' talent show. Essentially though, my work has changed to suit my life and my family. The best thing of all is that I decide those changes, and that's the key. Make your work work for you.

THANK YOU for me NOT having vertigo any more. Oh boy, that was bleddy awful. It started about two months into my UK tour. Something about the adrenalin, the raked (slanted) stage, and the very strong side lighting which we were forced to use (due to having a screen onstage that didn't work if light bounced directly on to it) set my neuro highways off, fizzing and confused. My eyes lied to my brain and told me that the floor was moving, that all straight lines were wobbly and that up was down. When it first happened, I thought something had 'popped' in my head and I felt very unsteady suddenly in the middle of a show in Worthing, on the pier. When the interval came, I told my crew to line up sidestage and drag me off when I toppled over as I felt certain that was going to happen. I asked for a chair to be set on the normally empty stage and I did the second half sitting down, the only place I felt safe. I saw a doc the following morning and hours later, I was inside an MRI machine, checking to see if I had a brain tumour or anything else similarly sinister.

Hold breath.

Hang on . . . might this be THAT moment . . .?

Oh God, am I OK?

Yep, all clear. And exhale . . .

Off to ear, nose and throat expert. Off to balance expert. Off to neurologist. Eventually I was diagnosed with Benign Positional Vertigo (not the kind you can cure by shaking your head vigorously, thanks anyway for the advice everyone!). It would remain with me for the best part of a year because the show itself was what exacerbated it. I was allergic to my show. I missed five shows while I was being treated. I'd never done that in thirty years so I resolved to finish the tour, including Australia, New Zealand and the West End. Sometimes I sat down, sometimes I took a walking stick on stage with me so I could steady myself. I constantly felt as if I would fall over, and I had to self-soothe, to talk myself through it. On several occasions, just before curtain up, I sat sidestage in tears, as my world was spinning so furiously that I was convinced I wouldn't remain upright for the duration of the show. That dreadful vertigo. The thief of my confidence, and of the fun of my show. Six weeks after I stopped performing it was gone, and I took my first deep breaths for a year. Good riddance.

THANK YOU for Cornwall and the chance, at last, to return home to live here ten years ago. Half of my family have Cornish roots, half have Devon roots, so I am mixed race and proud of it. I now live 200 yards from where my great-uncle ran his shop, thirty mins from my brother, thirty mins from Evil Granny's childhood haunts, and one minute forty seconds from my BF's house. Lovely.

The thing about Cornwall is that if it's in your blood, it never NEVER leaves you. The lure of it is potent. However much the county has its strife to deal with (and it does, it's a very poor ward), whoever you are, if you are in Cornwall, you are in the remarkable light. You are near the moors, the coves, the cliffs, the sea and the endless, endless sky. If you allow it, Cornwall will hold you in its gentle embrace, and that spectacular blue light will warm your bones and brighten some of your shadows. I know this to be true. Just as I know that Cornwall is also salty, strange, dark and blustery. I don't mind that. It keeps us on our toes, equal, nice and sharp. I have come home, summoned by pasties and cream, I have heeded that call. ONEN HAG OLL! One and all.

THANK YOU for optimism. I realize that, for years, I succumbed to the tyrannical notion that somehow cynicism is cool and optimism is cheesy. I now realize how misguided this is. It's a malaise. Cynicism, repeated and regular, is corrosive. It's the MO of snooty, lofty folk who believe that to sneer is to be clever. It's the place most people hide when they don't know what they think, or what they're talking about. I know that, because I used to be cynical when I felt exposed and vulnerable. It wasn't my true nature, but I tried it on for size for twenty years. It didn't suit OR fit me at all. In fact, it made me ill. Being snidey is a poison, however funny. And . . . is it really funny, even?

I used to curtail my optimism. No longer. Now I endeavour to find the good IF I can. It doesn't always work, like, for instance, the whole disappointing phenomenon that is the motorway service station. I approach them, actually turn off the motorway, every SINGLE time, with eternal optimism in my heart . . . what treats await me? What treasures? Perhaps a lovely sandwich? A new flavour of crisp? A hearty soup? A fragrant loo? The perfect coffee? And every SINGLE time, I am saddened, virtually to despair, by the reality I find. By the sheer lacklustre dullness. By the colour, the smell . . . the whole tawdry beige, two-for-one shebang. Dammit. I believed in you, Heston motorway service station   and you have disappointed me repeatedly. In your basket.

Still, despite such traumas, I refuse to cave in. I am endeavouring to stay sunny, focus more on the positive stuff, exercise my optimism muscle, and give the disappointments short shrift – unless of course they amuse me. Then the gloves are off.

'Comedy is simply a funny way of being serious'
Peter Ustinov

THANK YOU for dogs (and a little bit also for cats). Honestly, how delightful are they? Forget all the soppy fluffy girlie stuff. No anthropomorphizing. They have their own personalities and that's that. Dog personalities, not like ours. They have taught us to pander to their needs, not the other way round. I have spent endless hours of my life trying to get a dog to laugh. They do, sort of, but each of my dogs has found different stuff funny. Oh the joy when you discover the particular thing, and then you repeat it daily for fifteen years. The pleasure. The devotion. The comfort. (Don't bother trying to make a cat laugh, by the way. They don't stoop so low – they find comedy vulgar.)

I wish dogs lived longer. A small part of me has died with each one, and I reckon I only have enough of me left for one more dog . . . and one small cat.

THANK YOU to Philip Larkin for two things in particular. The first is his poem 'Born Yesterday', which he wrote for his new goddaughter. I am fortunate enough to have sixteen godchildren, and this poem truly says EVERYTHING they need to know about how it's OK to . . . be. I have quoted it on many occasions and it somehow gets truer.

Born Yesterday

Tightly-folded bud,
I have wished you something
None of the others would:
Not the usual stuff
About being beautiful,
Or running off a spring
Of innocence and love –
They will all wish you that,
And should it prove possible,
Well, you're a lucky girl.
But if it shouldn't, then
May you be ordinary;

Have, like other women,
An average of talents:
Not ugly, not good-looking,
Nothing uncustomary
To pull you off your balance,
That, unworkable itself,
Stops all the rest from working.
In fact, may you be dull –
If that is what a skilled,
Vigilant, flexible,
Unemphasised, enthralled
Catching of happiness is called.

And the other thing I thank Larkin for is the last line of his poem 'An Arundel Tomb': 'What will survive of us is love.' I choose to take this on its most simplistic and stark face-value, and I choose to believe it is right.

THANK YOU for meeting and marrying a lovely, faithful, kind, funny, selfless man, who appreciates and respects women.

No longer am I required to: wax or flirt, both of which I hate and am appalling at. I am now free to be my truest, most authentic, hairy, grumpy, big-pants-wearing self.

THANK YOU for:

Potatoes.

Bed.

Bras (putting on and especially taking off).

THANK YOU that I no longer have to:

Study for French A level.

Do cross country.

Wear high heels.

Kiss anyone who smokes.

THANK YOU, most of all, for my kids.

All three.

Extraordinary, interesting humans.

My purpose.

JUNE

monday »

tuesday »

wednesday »

thursday »

friday »

saturday »

sunday »

JUNE

monday »

tuesday »

wednesday »

thursday »

friday »

saturday »

sunday »

JUNE

monday »

tuesday »

wednesday »

thursday »

friday »

saturday »

sunday »

JUNE

monday »

tuesday »

wednesday »

thursday »

friday »

saturday »

sunday »

JUNE

monday »

tuesday »

wednesday »

thursday »

friday »

saturday »

sunday »

Contacts List
(one name per question)

- **The person** I could call in the middle of the night:

  ....

- **The person** that could call me in the middle of the night:

  ....

- **The person** that can make me laugh when I really need it:

  ....

- **The person** who can definitely keep a secret:

  ....

- **The person** I could be physically chained to for a whole year:

  ....

- **The person** whose advice I always listen to:

  ....

- **The person** whose advice I ought to listen to more:

  ....

- **The person** who, if I'm honest, I don't ALWAYS believe:

  ....

- **The person** whose wardrobe I'd like to steal:

  ....

- **The person** I would choose as my fantasy husband:

  ....

- **The person** I would choose as my fantasy wife:

  ....

- **The person** I would like to be my new best friend:

  ....

- **The person** I ought to tell the truth to:

  ....

JULY

'There is a crack in everything,
that's how the light gets in'
Leonard Cohen — 'Anthem'

I once knew a broken person whose name was Michelle. Back in the day, her kids, Yasmin and Sabrina, went to the same infant school as my young daughter. One day the headmistress asked me if I would consider picking them up each morning since their home was on my route to the school, and Michelle had no transport.

And so it started. Every day, I would pull in next to the flats where the three of them lived. I would sound the horn and the two girls would come out and jump in my car and off we would go. At first, the girls didn't speak much, and wouldn't maintain eye contact with me. My daughter asked me what was wrong, perhaps they didn't like us? We were a pretty rambunctious family after all, fairly noisy, singing along with the radio and inventing songs to learn times tables or spellings. Ours was not a quiet car. The girls kept themselves to themselves in the back, always polite, always reticent. They wouldn't be drawn into conversation much, they preferred to observe, and they kept their own counsel.

Gradually, as that first year ticked by, so the girls started to warm up a bit. It began with a few fleeting, furtive mutual glances in the rear-view mirror, and developed into the tiniest of smiles. I didn't push it; they were wary and cautious.

Michelle didn't seem to want to come out of her flat, so it was a while before I met her properly. Eventually she let me in the door, and I had more of an idea how this tight little family operated. It was immediately clear that Michelle was battling all kinds of demons, especially her own mental-health issues. She was a pretty woman, clearly a ghost of her former self, pale, nervous and wan. When she started to trust me, she opened up a bit about her fractured life in all its complexities, and I had a clearer picture of her inner warfare and how she saw the world as a sort of enemy who had it in for her. She was an intriguing mixture of fragile, furious and determined. At the heart of her chaotic life, though, lived an extraordinary power, the shining, unquestionable love she had for her two beautiful children. I saw her handle it all wrong many times, losing her patience or misunderstanding them or overreacting. I saw her make bad decisions. I saw her pull the curtains and withdraw into the gloom and occasionally forget to check if her kids were eating properly. I saw her become increasingly anxious, paranoid and thin.

All the while, the triumvirate of mother and daughters kept climbing the mountain that is trying daily to be a whole human. In time, the girls grew to trust us and have some fun. They were now a lovely addition to our family for the occasional day out/ cinema trip/lunch/party/sleepover, and they were growing, changing, blossoming, and trying to cope with school and exams and boys and life alongside the daily worry of having a mum who was in a total pickle, which regularly rendered her lost and hopeless. They were quietly magnificent throughout, constantly dodging all kinds of adult calamities they shouldn't have ever had to consider at their young age.

One day, when they were both teenagers, their shattered mum simply couldn't find the strength to fight on, and she took her own way out of her personal hell. With one step, she was free.

They, of course, were not.

They were hurled into a tornado of sorrow.

The reason I tell you this sad story is because it goes well beyond sadness. Although her life ended so tragically, it was lived with enormous courage. In order to just about function, Michelle had to go to war with her own state of mind every single day. There were many, many days when she wanted to bale out. She sometimes called me in the night, howling with the pain her tortured mind put her through, often begging me to take her kids, should she take herself that very night. I had to summon my own reserve tanks of considered judgement to challenge her with the fact that I would NOT be doing that, because SHE was going to carry on. To convince her that she was not insignificant or unloveable or a failure was hard, because she felt certain. Nevertheless, time after time, year after year, she somehow dredged up the strength to keep going. It was a daily battle to galvanize herself and defy her worst nightmares. She had to coax herself into any action whatsoever, she had to invent her own motivation. Something most of us don't have to consider at all. Whilst we were having our toast and tea in the mornings, she was regularly in the ring with two fierce opponents, shame and fear. She had to win that fight EVERY DAY in order to carry on. THAT is courage.

Her incentive was the love and pride she felt for those darling kids. She believed they were the only thing she did right in her life; she was ferociously proud of them and hugely protective in her own sometimes misguided way. They were considerate, hard-working, kind girls; they still are all that, and so much more.

The much more they are is extraordinary. To meet them, you wouldn't know the adversity they have survived. More than survived. Triumphed over. By rights, they shouldn't be able to smile so much, or be generous or forgiving. They shouldn't be able to make profound, trusting relationships where they are in turns vulnerable and resilient. Their own mental health probably shouldn't be in such good nick.

But it is.

Because they are the best of her. They are her strength and her awesome courage.

And they are their own complete selves.

Mighty young women, who have prevailed and who radiate love.

Who are supremely loveable, emotionally intelligent, beautiful and

KICK ASS!

We talk together about their mum Michelle sometimes, and as they have matured, they understand more about mental ill-health and its cruel grip. They have journeyed through anger and sorrow; they likely always will experience some remnants of that, but they have come to such a healthy place of acceptance. It's in that place that we are linked by the experience of a suicide parent. All three of us share the fact that we know we were loved and we know we have a future.

We are not their mistakes or their illness.

We are free of that.

We are entitled to LIFE.

We have their spirits as our fuel, and we can properly LIVE.

And we have each other to witness all those living moments. Passing exams, new jobs, new homes, graduations and weddings . . .

How proud their mum would have been on both of their wonderful wedding days, and how privileged was I to be there for her, and for them . . . and for me.

I suppose, really, that I write this in praise of the broken amongst us, and the broken in ourselves. We shouldn't be too quick to dismiss some of our bloody awful life experiences, despite how much we long to dump them and move on quickly. I have found that these difficulties have been my best opportunities for learning.

Let me say, also, that being affected vicariously by someone else's mental-health issues is very different to having your own, I know that. I'm not claiming to fully understand deep depression. I'm only claiming to have witnessed it. I once saw a quote which went something like this (sorry, I don't know who said it): 'Saying you understand chronic depression is like saying you've lived in Italy when actually you've only eaten at an Olive Garden Café.'

It's true of course.

There is still value to recognizing it, however. Or even in actively looking for it when your instincts tell you to do so. I am a great believer that what you ignore, you give permission to. I will never again ignore the sadness of someone close to me, or indeed, of anyone in my orbit. If I allow that, it can easily continue. I am very happy to be told to butt out if I am overstepping a boundary. I would rather risk that than be negligent of hidden suffering which so often parades as 'coping'. None of us asks for help easily. None. Certainly not me. Whereas most of us offer help easily.

Why? Is it status? Is it that we are so glad to not be in the position of need? Maybe. I would hope that if we are feeling strong and relatively mentally well, (whatever that is!) it's surely part of our job as interdependent, social humans to keep an eye out for someone who might be struggling. Bearing in mind our own knowledge of when we too have been in that position. We all have, in varying degrees.

I think of it in this way: people are like professionally polished rocks. If you hold one in your hand, the first thing you really see is the reflection of yourself. It's easy to look past the actual rock. In fact you don't properly see it at all until cracks appear and it breaks open. Then a whole other facet is revealed. Rough and real. The substrate. The authentic person who is, by then, a bit broken.

The fracturing is a relief sometimes. I know when I have felt profoundly sad in my life that the breaking moment can be the very opportunity to admit and accept, to allow the easement, to temporarily abandon the structures you've had to keep the façade in place. The scaffolding can remain, but the stone is cracked, the pointing needs attending to.

'Those who suffer much will know much'
Greek proverb

While we're in there, by the way, right in the hot core of difficulty, I'd also like to put a bid in for massive tolerance of inconsistency and occasional outbursts of downright hypocrisy! We are, after all, in a kind of altered state when we're injured. It's OK to be a bit weird while we work through it. Let's be tender with the broken and let's be tender with the broken in ourselves.

JULY

monday »

. . . .

tuesday »

. . . .

wednesday »

. . . .

thursday »

. . . .

friday »

saturday »

sunday »

JULY

monday »

tuesday »

wednesday »

thursday »

friday »

saturday »

sunday »

JULY

monday »

tuesday »

wednesday »

thursday »

friday »

saturday »

sunday »

JULY

monday »

tuesday »

wednesday »

thursday »

friday »

saturday »

sunday »

JULY

monday »

....

tuesday »

....

wednesday »

....

thursday »

....

friday »

saturday »

sunday »

The Things That Can F**k Right Off

- Adult colouring books
- Cystitis
- Saying 'could of' instead of 'could have'
- Courgette spaghetti
- Trump and all who sail in him
- Bullies (see above)
- Contouring
- Kardashians
- Cancer
- Anyone who doesn't like children
- Alzheimer's
- Saying, 'I'm not racist, but . . .'
- Saying, 'That's me for you'
- Loud chewing
- Cold sores
- Body shaming
- Eyelashes on car headlights
- Hygge
- Underwired bras
- Nylon pants
- Nylon sheets
- Nylon
- Daddy long legs
- Brexit
- Cold callers
- Blue cheese (BLUE?! CHEESE?!)
- Orange juice with the bits still in

Please extend the list yourself . . .

- ....
- ....
- ....
- ....
- ....
- ....
- ....
- ....
- ....
- ....
- ....
- ....
- ....
- ....
- ....
- ....
- ....
- ....

AUGUST

HOLIDAYS!

As I circle my sixtieth birthday, I think about the different kinds of holidays I've had at various times in my life.

HOLIDAYS WITH MUM, DAD AND BROTHER WHEN I WAS A LITTLE KID

Main memories: in an anorak, looking at old castles in Scotland.

In an anorak, working the locks on the River Trent.

In an anorak, endlessly looking in rockpools in Cornwall.

HOLIDAYS WITH FRIENDS IN MY TEENS AND TWENTIES

Main memories: staying in cheap hostels and catching fleas, pubic lice and athlete's foot (better than pubic foot and athlete's lice, I suppose. . .).

Continuously counting money to be able to get to the last day, and to the airport, only to find there's an airport tax I can't afford.

Disastrously misreading the signs from several travelling companion chaps and discovering that a) they don't fancy me, so there will be no romance, or b) they're gay, so there will be no romance, or c) for no discernible reason, save our mutual awkwardness, there will simply be no romance.

Thinking that slathering my entire body with chip fat stolen from the hostel will make great sunscreen.

Crying at Pompeii, when I saw the petrified remains of a lava-preserved child.

Wishing we could sit down and watch people, more than walk around and see things.

Eating five FAB ice lollies every day for a week on the beach at Gwithian.

Fumbly sex in sweaty tents.

HOLIDAYS WITH LOVERS AND PARTNERS

Main memories: realizing on day ONE in Greece that this particular boyfriend is so very, very unsuitable, therefore working out how to render him physically and mentally incapable by 9 p.m. each evening.

Deploying cheap industrial cooking brandy to this end.

Making the fatal mistake of attempting some patois in Jamaica in a desire to be 'cool'. Subsequently experiencing the stinging thrum of laughter at my back. Massively uncool.

Feeling so grown up, being alone with a handsome man on a beach, on a holiday we paid for with dosh made from telling silly jokes, dressing up and showing off.

Being in charge of the passports and the tickets. Yes. There were such things.

Coming to the sobering conclusion that I will never ever wear a spaghetti strap (not real spaghetti) sleeveless dress. Ever. Not even on a warm evening.

Realizing I will never go out braless. Ever.

Noticing that other women do and being in awe. Awe that teeters dangerously on the edge of jealousy and low self-esteem ... and then plonks itself back firmly on the solid ground of simple curiosity and respect. It's OK to be different to them and it's OK to have big bosoms. In fact, it's great.

Wanting very much for my chap to swim with me in the warm Mediterranean Sea. He ALWAYS wanted to read instead, and only swim when everyone else was gone and in his own time. I once swam out into the bay and called for him to join me. He shook his head and I knew then, in an instant of utter surety, that I couldn't be with him any more. The tipping point. When you just know.

More fumbly sex in sweaty tents.

HOLIDAYS WITH FAMILY AND LITTLE KIDS

Main memories: taking it in turns to deal with the night shift alongside a bolt-awake jet-lagged tot.

Trying to explain how different toilets are in other countries.

Being terrified when my three-year-old's asthma took a turn for the worse on holiday with a friend in Minorca. She quickly deteriorated and went limp in my arms. I had to speak in Spanish to a doctor on the phone urgently to get directions to an all-night chemist and to explain what was happening. I don't speak any Spanish, but I somehow did that night.

Getting henna tattoos from hippies on the pavement in Corfu. Letting my daughter have one of a dolphin on her arm. Watching her allergy to it angrily blister up and get infected. She still has traces of it today. Some people's skin doesn't like henna.

Games around the table with lots of kids. Making up new words, especially swear words, and finding out what everyone's last meal might be, and which Spice Girl they are going to marry in twenty years' time. Most wanted to marry Baby, because she was voted 'the kindest'. Even the girls thought she would be the best option for them, except a few renegades who voted for Gaston from *Beauty and the Beast*, mainly because of his remarkable arms. Concur.

No sex. Too knackered. Too sunburnt. Kids in bed.

HOLIDAYS WITH ADULT KIDS

Main memories: the absolute need to behave like much littler kids at the airport, mainly in the lounge, mainly due to massive over-excitement.

'Stealing' the in-flight wash kits and feeling mighty fortunate.

Late-night fire on the beach in New Zealand.

Cooking sausages on sticks in the flames.

Ghost stories.

Catastrophizing in Mexico, imagining that when they went off into town for an evening, some cartel member would SURELY plant class A drugs on them and we'd spend the next five years fighting to get them out of Mexican jail, having to sell our house to fund the court cases. Yeah. Chilled in Mexico . . .

That moment on a beach where you look over and see him next to you, and beyond him, her, and her, and him. Five sausages frying in the same heat, dopey and safe. Family together, with only mojitos in mind. Bliss.

HOLIDAYS WITH JUST YOUR DARLIN'

Main memories: him with 'binokliers' checking for pirates/whales/birds of exceptional beauty.

Trusting that food in wayside cafes in far-off distant countries is actually for human consumption. Knowing in your heart, on this one occasion, it isn't.

Staying up 'til 4 a.m. binge-watching *House of Cards*. 'Being' the ruthless Francis and Clare when making late-night sandwiches or toast, just to experiment with what it feels like to prepare snacks when you have no soul.

Holding hands on tiny planes seemingly made of paper, flown by teenagers not concentrating on keeping them in the air. Wondering if this level of bum-twinking fear is part of being a well-travelled person?

Reading books in easy silence. Swapping books. Muscular debate about books. Abandoning the swapped book, reclaiming the original one, and more reading, but now in less easy silence . . .

Planning a new dog. Thinking of names, including 'Satan', 'Nits' and 'Susan' . . . Having a scary thought flash through my mind, might this be my last dog . . .? Blimey. Tick. Tock.

Sometimes it's only when you're on holiday and your mind is rested and open enough that these bigger thoughts can seep in. There's a danger with deep thinking, in that if you don't get the chance to do it much, you can mistake it for the truth, as if the truth is only plumbed in the bottomless moments. I think it's often only the loudest thoughts that are heard in quiet minutes, not necessarily the truest.

I like to think that I am the more authentic me when I am relaxed; that I am who I most am then. Perhaps though, it's simply that there's time to reflect. I'm too busy most of the time, like all of us, to judge myself. Too busy and not bothered enough. I think that's why I sometimes surprise myself on holiday, with how anxious or grumpy or plain odd I can be. I have been known to take advantage of the precious time available to treat myself to a really satisfying extensive lemon-lipped sulk, typically about a relatively minor thing. It's partly because there is time to devote to it, and partly because it's interesting to explore the sulky state at leisure. It's a childish, indulgent thing to do and it's relatively ugly in so many ways, but it's almost as if it flushes your emotional system out.

Who hasn't, when on holiday, decided that on reflection, EVERYTHING in their house at home is hideous and that, yes indeed, the entire dark teak, fancy woodwork, colourful throws and pom-pom mirrors of a Balinese interior is the way forward? I know I have. I have shipped home huge quantities of entirely unsuitable furniture at great expense only to find a) it doesn't fit in or suit my house, and b) identical items are found at Habitat for a quarter of the price. I saw them there last year, thanks, and didn't like them then . . . so why have I BOUGHT THEM NOW?!!?

Who hasn't, when on holiday, decided quite categorically that you definitely want to move to this country to live, or, at the very least, buy a home here to come to on your holidays? Furthermore, when you return home, you are going to CHANGE YOUR WHOLE LIFE, and take loads more holidays . . . like, maybe eight a year . . . or something . . . so that you can come here at any time. Pretty much two days after your return home, all of these seismic decisions are as air . . . forgotten, gone.

Who hasn't, whilst on holiday, felt like the two weeks just AREN'T ENOUGH, that it's all going to whizz past far too quickly . . . and then felt the day before returning home that it's been far too long and that you're longing to be back home? Back where you understand everything, however irritating, back where you're more familiar with yourself.

With your flawed, flummoxed self.

Yep.

Home.

Lovely.

AUGUST

monday »

tuesday »

wednesday »

thursday »

friday »

saturday »

sunday »

AUGUST

monday »

tuesday »

wednesday »

thursday »

friday »

saturday »

sunday »

AUGUST

monday »

tuesday »

wednesday »

thursday »

friday »

saturday »

sunday »

AUGUST

monday »

tuesday »

wednesday »

thursday »

Aged 15

friday »

saturday »

sunday »

AUGUST

monday » ....

tuesday » ....

wednesday » ....

thursday » ....

friday »

saturday »

sunday »

Reference Letter

Recently I was asked to write a reference letter for someone who had worked for me for seven years. It was a fascinating exercise. What to say? What not to say? How to convey in a formal way the nature, the character, the heart and the truth of a person. I wondered if I could do it of myself ...?

Across is a space to write your letter, recommending yourself and giving reasons why.

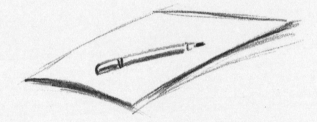

To Whomsoever It May Concern:

Take a picture of yourself as you are right now,

and place it here.

AUTUMN

If you are 50-75 years old, you will recognize at least half of the following:

- Politicians/dentists/policemen + women seem ridiculously young

- You have a favourite cup/plate/crockery

- You turn the plugs off at the wall at night

- You go carefully down the stairs

- You refuse to 'wear in' shoes

- Your date of birth seems a long time away and sounds massively old-fashioned

- People are interested in talking to you about 'your era'

- You have to make lists

- You love routine

- You are interested in ancestry and genealogy

- You have a 'signature dish' (see later)

- You have a ridiculously sweet tooth

- You are overzealous about the music you love

- Your torso is thickening

- You constantly feel, 'This can't be happening to me, surely?', about any health issues

- You love a sneaky nap

- You begrudge filling out the over-fifty part of any health/insurance form

Here we are, in the full drama of Nature's act III, where the colours make lots of noise. Big bold shouty crimsons, russets, oranges, yellows and browns all compete to be heard in their flourish of a fanfare, the final shout before they leave the show, exiting stage left pursued by a naughty wind, hamming it up all the way. Autumn resolutely refuses to be upstaged by Spring when it comes to display. She has fat apples and dark swollen blackberries and rosehips and elderflowers to offer as her treasures during this transforming time, when day and night agree to be the same length again, and when:

- spiderwebs are bedecked with dew
- spiders head indoors. Eeek!
- flies die
- wasps disappear
- honey is harvested
- logs and coal are ordered
- we stop cutting the grass
- stags are rutting
- porridge and stew and pumpkin soup are on the table
- birds fly away
- we make chutney
- hops are picked
- clocks go back
- Halloween and Diwali happen
- new school shoes are bought
- there's smoke in the chimneys
- it rains rude, thick rain

We put our clocks back and dread the weight of Winter for the first time this year, and then we remember, oh hang on, it ain't so bad, this means there'll be candles at dinner time, and we love that . . .

We cry at Harvest Festivals in junior schools where tiny tots learn about gathering in all the fruit and vegetables grown throughout the Summer by cramming misbought tins of strange beans into shoeboxes that will be given to the elderly or the needy who will most probably recycle them exactly the same way next year. The tables and altars will heave with ornamental sheaves of bread and a cornucopia of berries and fruit, and we will feel fortunate and fed.

Oh, and the unmistakeable smell synonymous with Autumn. What is it really? A mixture of overripe fruit, rotting leaves, fireworks, mud, frost, smoke and rain. Everything seems earthy, probably because wherever there are trees there is now mulch underfoot, nourishing the ground beneath, where beetles and millipedes and millions of other crawlies are gorging on delicious leafy debris. Even fungi are feasting on the sweet rot. It's so . . . damn . . . more-ish . . .

September is soft, almost sad, and beckons us indoors to start our withdrawal. As the shorter days creep in, so too do we retreat gently, into a familiar seasonal kind of melancholy. The days pull back, we pull in, and we take our comforts in the welcoming warm places inside us. We feel homesick and nostalgic and ready to settle, and let our bums get a bit broad in a comfy armchair. It's not a surrender, we're not going to seed, it's just a rest and a pleasure.

Presently, I am firmly IN this season of my life. I am sixty. When I was a child, I genuinely thought it might be better if everyone aged sixty or over was just . . . gently, discreetly, killed. Because what is the point of them? They are nearly dead anyway and why prolong the inevitable decrepitude? Well, I didn't think in terms of decrepitude exactly, but you know what I mean . . . I thought sixty was ancient, elderly, infirm.

And here I am, alive and really well. Aliver and weller, ironically, than I was in my forties, when I was often considering my age, my place in my lifespan and my uncertain future. I gave inordinate power to anxious thinking back then. I don't any more. Well, I do less. I think I tired of myself as a constant seeker, I wanted to slide into the role of a finder, instead; it's more assured, it fits me loads better. In order to do that, I have had to allow myself quietude to reflect and properly re-group, to 'move my chair into sun'. Only in my fifties have I been calm enough to do that. It's second nature, which in turn means it's natural, which in turn means it's normal.

Perhaps that's the true purpose of this 'middle age'? Actually, hang on, when IS middle age?! And how long does it last for? Sixty can't be middle-aged, I'm surely deluded, otherwise we'd all be living 'til we are a hundred and twenty or something. So, is middle age the actual middle of your life? And if we're all living much longer, is that say, fifty? Or is it forty? Is it an age or a state of mind? If it's the latter, I need to do some serious re-thinking because I haven't felt like I've exited middle age yet. And, if I have, what have I entered? OLD age?! Blimey. Heck. And bollox.

You know that moment when you stand back and notice who else is your age? It's always a tad surprising. I went to a school reunion quite a few years ago, and for a good five minutes I was convinced that my old chums had sent their mums along instead. Here were some women in A-line skirts, tan tights and court shoes. They looked a bit like the people I once knew, but they had morphed into their darlin' mothers. Not all of them, of course, just a few, but it was shocking. MORE shocking though, was when I caught sight of myself in the mirror, and realized that I was one of them! Maybe not so much with the clobber, but certainly with my mother's face. Do I really mind? No, my mum had a lovely face. It's just that, as I remember it, it was mostly seventy-seven years old.

I have been delighted to find that, give or take a few silly years, I am the same age as Ellen DeGeneres, Kim Cattrall, Oprah Winfrey and, oh my goodnessing heck ... MADONNA.

That's THE Madonna, the Mother of Lourdes.

Not any old Madonna, the Mother of Christ.

I mean the actual, real, authentic one, the Material Girl, the undisputed Queen of Pop, the true artist. There are only half a million inconsequential minutes between our dates of birth, so I am taking that to mean that we are virtually twins, and, as such my twin heart breaks vicariously a little bit every time she is age-shamed. She can get older any way she ruddy likes, can't she? When she was bullied again recently by a bloke in a newspaper, she wrote,

```
'How do I know I'm still acting my Age? Because it's MY
age and it's MY life and all of you Women Hating Bigots
need to sit down and try to understand why you feel the
       need to limit me with your fear of what you aren't
                   familiar with.'
```

That's right, sista. Sadly, we are all too unfamiliar with strong, sexually confident empowered older women displaying their assurance as she does, unashamedly.

Now, talk of Madge brings me on to the prickly puffy phenomenon that is plastic surgery. Not that I know if she has travelled that particular route, I haven't yet received a memo about it, so I don't really know for sure if she's had a tidy, but . . . I suspect so. It's ABSOLUTELY NONE OF MY EFFING BUSINESS of course when it concerns her, but it definitely IS my business when it concerns me. The awful truth is that when you're sixty, and especially if you're in the business of show, it is utterly expected of you to resort to knives or injections in an effort to stem the inevitable tide of age flooding your face with crinkly bits. Thus far I have resisted but I would fight to the bloody death for Madge, or anyone else, to do what we like to our own mug, if we choose to.

EXCEPT. Hmmmm . . .

DO we choose to? Or are we women all bullied so atrociously much about our appearance that, to fend off the criticism, WE are prepared to voluntarily mutilate ourselves so that we can appear a tiny bit younger? This fleeting and desperate measure means we can stave off feeling ugly or somehow lesser than we are 'supposed' to be, for a few paltry months more. As sure as chickens are chickens, and eggs are crow's feet, age is coming for us all and it's armed with wrinkles and sag and droop and spread. None of it is pleasant, and when it starts to happen, it's with alarming speed . . . BUT . . . that's the natural order. That's what is supposed to happen. Give me that ordinary decay in all its infernal inevitability any day over the monstrous barbarism which presents itself as the eminent plastic surgeons' apparent 'skill'. Why have so many breathtakingly beautiful people ended up so woefully injured? And, somehow, we have normalized this. We say, 'Hello, how are you?' to folk who we rightly should be screaming in horror for, offering them an ambulance and a good lawyer for the lamentable disfiguring that has been wrought upon them in the name of beauty. For shame. For all our collective shame.

I fear that we have come to accept these vandalized faces as indicators of wealth and status, of someone who is 'taking the trouble' to attend to their appearance; of someone who welcomes the attack, despite the result.

If that is so, then I am simply too lazy to attempt to remain young-looking. Or too afraid of the obvious mistakes that clearly happen very often. Look at the poor wretches with the gone-wrong faces! Why are the surgeons not in rat-infested prisons for their heinous crimes?! Instead of driving boasty Porsches?

Of course, I refer to the obvious horrors. I presume that the clever, subtle work is undetectable and thus I wouldn't know it. Good. THAT is skill. The rest is butchery and I can't accept that it's OK, and I won't pretend, otherwise by the time my daughters are thirty, they will be being given facial surgery vouchers as birthday gifts.

NO.

NO.

NO.

And there's an end on it.

(Cut to picture of me on a red carpet with a face like a cheap overstuffed button-backed headboard and wearing my fanny as a beard).

Never mind believing that being sixty is practically the end as I did when I was younger, would the teenage Dawn ever have imagined that I would be starting a whole new chapter of my life in my mid-fifties? No. Neither would the twenty-, thirty- or even forty-year-old Dawn. I have always been quite a dogged person. If I make a promise, my sense of resolution firmly kicks in and I remain steadfast. Marriage is a promise, a huge promise, and I didn't make it lightly. I was an ex-Brownie after all, used to blind dedication. I was determined to make it work, come hell or high water. Then some hell DID come, followed by some high water, and I still lingered. No-one wants to fail at an important relationship, but I decided that instead of thinking of it as 'failing' the marriage, I would instead be surviving, and thus bettering my life. The only way to do that was with honesty, kindness and grace, with the odd touch of vitriolic fury at appropriate moments, in the company of the right people. In other words, the way for me to handle this and many other tricky situations is and always has been to face it head on, the Roma French way:

'The only way out is through.'

While I was doing that, going through the process of hurt and anger and forgiveness, and finally acceptance, SO MUCH was going on for me that I was utterly unaware of. I was gradually, subconsciously, coming to realize such a lot.

I didn't want to waste another single moment of my life sitting passively in a wrong situation, misguidedly waiting for it to right itself.

I didn't want to compromise so much that I lost sight of myself a bit.

I didn't want to ever ignore constant inner instincts, I want to be alert to them.

I want to reassess who and what I deserve, and who and what deserves me.

I want to somehow forgive the mistakes of the past, both mine and other sundry twots, so that the way ahead is lovely and clear:

I want to be like Elsa, and 'let it go' (on the understanding that I DON'T want to be like Elsa and have a waist smaller than my neck, otherwise how do you eat doughnuts?).

I want to live comfortably IN my authentic self, no apologies, no faking, live where I am, in what I am.

I want to notice what I have denied myself and work out why, with little/no (all right, some) bitterness.

I want my milkshake to bring all the boys to the yard. Damn right...

I want to hurry up and be better at everything.

I want to work out the right vitamins to take.

I want to finally capitulate and admit that it's all about the bass...no treble.

I want to ALWAYS live by the sea, please.

So, you see, whilst I was dealing with the difficult logistical surface stuff of a divorce, my heart was faithfully sorting out all of the above and gradually, the confusing haze of trauma lifted, and I had a brighter, happier place in my sights as my focus.

'In a dark time, the eye begins to see ...'
T. Roethke

During my reacquaintance with my newly single self, I had the rare opportunity to plug in properly to my friends,

Ah. My friends.

Thank you, God, or whoever, for all the right stuff they said and did.

The one who MOVED IN WITH ME to be there to listen to every repeated bleating lament.

The one who reminded me that kindness is like a torch; if you shine it into shadowy corners, it chases away the dark.

The one who cooked hot Thai broth for me.

The one who packed me off to the best gynaecologist in town, no ifs or buts. Just in time, as it happens.

The one who lay next to me and whispered, 'I'm here, I've got you, I'll breathe with you 'til it's easy.'

The one who invited me to all of their family dinners.

The one who made beetroot cake.

The one who walked on the beach with me, in all weathers.

The one who crawled into my bed to be there when I woke up.

The one who drove 200 miles to say Happy Birthday.

The one who reminded me to say 'YES' more often.

The one who reorganized my food cupboards with military precision.

The one who made me a bath with excess bubbles.

The one who told me to butch up.

The one who said we would love each other 'til our last breaths.

The one who dragged me out to watch drag.

The one who told me to treat my heart as if it had been stabbed and let it have time to heal.

The one who bought tickets for Dolly Parton.

The one who read to me.

The one who was almost violent in her ferociously protective advocacy.

The ones who quietly, subtly, became my tribe, and surrounded me with their patient understanding.

All of these selfless souls took the time to support me in so many different, sometimes alarming (!) ways and I was reminded daily that I wasn't alone, that I am part of a firmament of family and friends, all of us connected inextricably to each other under a big wide sky. They weren't about to let me fall. Their love shored me up, and touched me very deeply. These people, my beloved friends, are my foundation. These are the relationships that will endure. These are the strong emotional bequests I will certainly try to pass on, on my climb towards the mountain.

Oh yes, that mountain. Here at sixty years old I'm aware that my climb is well underway. In fact, if I stop occasionally to look, I can see that I've travelled much further up it and, believe me, the view is starting to be pretty spectacular, even though the ascent is puffing me out!

From this place on the mountain in my life, a couple of things strike me as pretty much given.

By now, I know it is all right to draw some conclusions and to have an opinion, yes, but the most useful lesson I have learnt is that it's also all right to doubt it and also to change it.

I also know that most of the stuff in my life thus far that has really pained me, has been because I've taken it personally when, on reflection, I really didn't need to. Note to sixty-year-old self.

I know that at this stage, I can pretty much say, 'This is who I am.' A lot of my personal ingredients have already been partially cooked, but I'm not ready quite yet, I've still got a slightly soggy bottom.

Nevertheless, 'This is who I am right now'. Yes.

I know that life is composed of various delights and riches with the odd irksome tribulation thrown in. One of those tribulations needs to be highlighted. It is the curse that is *Kummerspeck*. Heard of it?

Kummerspeck – the German for the excess weight gained from emotional overeating. Literally, it translates as 'grief bacon'.

Now let's get one thing quite clear. I've been a big girl and woman my whole life. Sometimes bigger, sometimes less big. Typically, the differing bigness didn't necessarily correlate to my emotional state. I've been bigger when at my happiest and similarly the converse is also true. I simply won't have it that sadness and fat go neatly together, it's much more complicated than that . . .

BUT . . .

After my mum died in my mid-fifties, I definitely found my comforts in certain kinds of eating I hadn't hitherto been familiar with, like . . . the world of melted cheese (on everything including crisps and chicken) and the world of Magnum ice creams (sometimes with melted cheese). Oh lawd. Thanks, cheese and ice cream, for the genuine numbing of grief, but, frankly, that will be all. We're done here. Move along, grief bacon. I'm going to have the grief without the side order of emotional gristle, ta.

I know, too, that here in my coming sixties when I still have my health relatively intact, is my finest opportunity to kick up some Autumn leaves in my life, have a laugh, learn some new things from the young people around me, enjoy the loud beautiful colours, and be where I belong to be.

Right here.

Right now.

Things I Will Always Remember:

1. Grandma French's beautiful, kind old face.

2. The taste and size of Wagon Wheels at playtime.

3. Completely lying on top of Grandad's dog, Carlo the Alsatian.

4. My baby daughter's eyes looking up at me during a 3 a.m. feed.

5. My baby daughter's face when I let her suck on a Mars Bar for the first time . . .

6. The smell of newspaper ink and paperboys in the early morning at my grandparents' newsagent shop.

7. The excitement of Christmas Eve when I was seven years old.

8. The smell of my mum's chest.

9. My dad's haunted face the last time I saw him.

10. Magnified sunlit skin pores on my hand through snorkel-goggles underwater in Cyprus, 1964.

11. The terror of seeing *The Exorcist*.

12. The rows of dolls in national dress in Grandma's loft.

13. Choosing an engagement ring in Tiffany's on Fifth Avenue in New York aged nineteen.

14. The way five-year-old kids like to cling on to your neck if you are their teacher and you're telling a story.

15. My daughter's voice when she sang a cappella at our wedding.

16. Doing a radio interview in a small studio alongside an unknown Gregory Porter . . . who then sang. Two foot from my head. Realizing some people's gift is sacred.

Now, things you will always remember:

1. ....

2. ....

3. ....

4. ....

5. ....

6. ....

7. ....

8. ....

9. ....

10. ....

SEPTEMBER

There was a man in my family who carried his shame in a knapsack on his back, a boulder so heavy it created his own personal grim gravity. He was exhausted from having to pretend there was no such weight there. He wanted folk to believe his knapsack contained sandwiches and a thermos and some feathers, rather than the misery monolith it truly was. One day, he decided it was too heavy to carry, so he took it off and emptied it out. Shame. All over the floor, but not on him any more. He put the knapsack back on, empty and light, and he walked forward. Determined never to fill it again . . .

In my experience, shame is the most emotionally debilitating demon imaginable. It destroys our self-esteem and, all the time, we fake it. We grit our teeth and smile on through. Shame is invisible, but it is a fiercesome powerful ol' presence. The shame in me recognizes the shame in you, instantly feels ashamed and scoots off to hide from both of us. We fear that our shame is obvious, that we will see it reflected back. We fear it so much that we let it burrow into our hearts like a vile worm. The only way out is to own up to it, confront it and cast it aside. So easily said and THE MOST DIFFICULT THING TO DO. It takes so much courage, in fact, that it's often preferable to continue on, being eaten.

I have no easy answer to this, but I do know something for sure . . . get it out of you, because it is toxic, keeps you separate and will hurt you and those you love.

I've learnt that it's possible to encapsulate the shame we store in as few as two sentences. Just as a start. Try it. Go on.

Speak it aloud. Put it in the air.

Then think about who you could speak it aloud TO. Someone safe, who will hear it right.

Just consider it.

Just consider it.

Just do it ...?

Two sentences and it could, just might be, the start of a new different, less-shame-thank-you way of being. Contempt is a weighty ol' burden, and it gets heavier the longer you harbour it. So often, the confusion and the feelings of inadequacy are bound up in one type of utterly damning thinking which has 'I am bad' at its core, when really 'I think I have done something bad' is more accurate. And infinitely more manageable.

Feeling a sense of shame about yourself, to whatever degree, is pretty normal, I reckon, sadly. That's hard enough to deal with. It's a big life battle, a part of adulthood.

The more worrying, and for me fairly unforgivable trait, is in those who, commonly as a reaction to their own shame-pain, decide to consciously assign shame to others. When shame is heaped upon you, when it makes no sense to you, when it's somehow ascribed to you, THAT'S when it becomes a ruddy monster, that s when it smashes you up. An inexplicable beast, which in your deepest, most difficult, vulnerable place, you somehow believe you DESERVE to be savaged by.

Ummmmmm ...? NO!

What you DESERVE,

What all of us DESERVE ...

Is to be treated with respect, as equals.

I expect that of others towards me, so in my most serious and difficult moments, I try to remember that I need to treat myself just the same. To do that, I absolutely have to shun any unwarranted shame that's being donated from dubious quarters. No thanks. Not available for that, got plenty of my own stuff to sort, don't need extra.

Blimey, it's ruddy difficult knowing how to be a functioning human, isn't it?

How do you be a good person?

How do you be a person?

How do you be?

How do you successfully be a wife, a mother, a sister, a friend, a daughter, all rolled into one?

I don't really know, but at least I know I don't totally know, and I know not to pretend I know when I don't. HA!

I also know that not everything has a solution, so I shouldn't always be looking to fix stuff if that is not possible. I can't change how other people are, or the choices they make or the consequences of those choices: all I can do is witness those things and change the way I deal with them if needs be. I can also admit that I will sometimes get it monumentally wrong, I will doubt myself and I will worry, but, that's all right.

'Where doubt is, there truth is — it is her shadow'
Ambrose Bierce

I am the sort of person who likes to tackle things head-on, I like all the cards on the table so that I know exactly what I'm dealing with. This can lead me into trouble and has done before now. I can be a bit of a gun-jumper, a bit impatient with my need to get to the truth, often sooner than some people are prepared to. I know that. My best friend is supremely subtle and goes about her life carefully, sensitively. I admire it, I do . . . but I just can't do it. Well, that's a lie, I don't WANT to do it, that's the truth. I want to deal with the difficult stuff, right NOW. To prolong it is agony for me, however prudent it might be.

I hope that I am honest, at least with myself. I don't feel that I have to spill my guts about everything to everyone, but if I do spill 'em, I'll be telling the truth. Whatever 'the truth' is. I realize it can be different for everyone. I am referring to my own truths, however unpalatable or shameful they may sometimes be.

It's different if you have blockages that somehow prevent you from getting on with life, especially if you can't quite identify them. You know the kind of disquiet I mean – it's there in the pit of your belly when you wake in the night but you're not exactly sure what it is. A kind of anxiety indigestion. The ghost of an unsettled score you can't quite grasp. You can't fathom it: what is nibbling away at your calm?

If you truly don't know, as opposed to hiding away from it, then you have to get a helping hand to unpick it, from someone who knows what they're up to.

When I was in my forties, I sought out some help to deal with a nagging, dreadful sadness that was bugging me. After seeing a very clever psychologist for a few months, and talking through some of the inner turbulence I was experiencing, she suggested that I might try a therapy called EMDR. I thought at first she was suggesting drugs of some sort, and that's not my bag, unless it's totally unavoidable of course. She quickly explained that it was nothing to do with chemicals. The letters stand for Eye Movement Desensitization and Reprocessing.

I know . . .

WHAT ...?!

She went on to explain that this type of therapy was quite new, but that in her opinion, it was very effective in treating trauma. She said that if something shocking has happened to you, your brain tries to process the shock of it, usually with rapid eye movements while you're asleep. All humans do this, actually even dogs do it. How phenomenal is that? Well, sometimes your brain fails to sort the shock into its correct drawer in your head, or maybe the shock is so powerful, it resists the unconscious processing, so, instead, you actively do the sorting while you are awake, mimicking the eye movements in your conscious state.

WHAT ...?!

She went on to tell me that she suspected she knew from listening to me for weeks where my particular mental hurdles were, and so what would happen was this:

She would sit in front of me, and by following her fingers rhythmically, waving from side to side, my eyes would move just as they needed to. During this, she would be talking me carefully through a particular memory that she knew was difficult for me. A moment that was emotionally charged and particularly disturbing. She would attempt to have me recall it in detail and slowly, working together, she would guide me to a different type of thinking around it, to a better, more positive take on it.

WHAT ...?!

She told me straight away that, knowing me, she imagined I might find it all a bit absurd. I might laugh, or scoff at it and even dismiss it completely, and that was natural and OK. It couldn't hurt me. It was worth trying.

So I did. For ninety minutes or so, I recounted the incident she wanted me to retell. She encouraged me to be brave and forensic with the details of it. All the while, she skilfully nudged me onwards, and she gently moved her fingers in front of me like a metronome. Left, right. Left, right. Once I got past the ridiculous feeling of being hypnotized in some Victorian freak show, I relaxed into it, and before too long my face was wet with tears as I told my upsetting story. Left, right, left, right. As I spoke, I knew the weight of it was gradually lifting, even in that very first session. I was spent at the end of it, completely wrung out. I went home and dreamt vivid dreams, and when I woke up, I swear the edges of that knobbly old sadness were definitely knocked off. I could remember it clearly as before but, unlike before, it didn't hurt as much. It simply didn't matter in the same awful way; the power of it was dampened.

I had a couple more sessions of that same treatment, and within a month I was sleeping properly again and the whole damn difficult thing was nicely filed away where it should be. On the back burner, so to speak. Not the front burner, where it was burning me.

I'm told that this type of therapy is most effective with people who have had huge hissing traumas. Folk who've been to war, who've been raped, who've been in car accidents, appalling stuff like that. I can believe it, because it worked so well for me, whose trauma was minor in comparison.

How wonderful is the human mind? How elastic and interesting? Look how it rights itself, given half a chance. It's miraculous. Whoever invented it should really have a jelly and a badge. Or two jellies, even.

At the centre of the success of that type of treatment is, essentially, trust.

I had to trust her.

I had to trust the process.

I had to trust my brain.

I had to trust myself.

It's a risk, isn't it, trusting? A risk we absolutely HAVE to take if we don't want to end up alone and isolated. A risk we have to take repeatedly, even after our trust is violated. The only way we can guarantee never to be let down is never to trust. No thanks.

Ernest Hemingway said,

> 'The best way to find out if you can trust anybody
> is to trust them.'

Trusting is tricky for a person who likes to be in the driver's seat, like me. Trust is about being in the passenger's seat. With the maps and the sweets. It's about allowing someone else to drive YOUR car. And not just in terms of romantic relationships, but in every truthful, valuable human relationship we make. We trust people all the time.

We trust our friends will keep our secrets.

We trust our wine isn't watered down.

We trust our dog won't bite that new puppy down the road (misplaced trust).

We trust our kids will remember the lessons we taught them to keep them safe.

We trust our hearts in each other's keep.

We trust other drivers to stop at a red light.

We trust our instincts.

We trust that humanity is essentially good.

We trust that our families have our backs.

We trust our pants to stay up.

We trust our comedy partner to remind us of the line when we forget it in front of 4,000 people.

One of the giant rewards for learning, gradually, to trust more and more as you travel through your life, is that more and more, people trust you. In that single privilege, I find huge happiness. The beauty of it, of someone believing you are trustworthy. It's good, it's really good. Being a safe place for someone, for anyone, is a proper grown-up responsibility, one to relish.

So, I am stepping forward into September, refusing to let shame be in charge of anything and allowing trust to flourish. My September is shame-less and trust-full.

Owzyours?

1 Things I am ashamed of:

_____

_____

_____

_____

_____

· ·

2 Things I am proud of:

_____

_____

_____

_____

_____

· ·

3 Things/people I don't trust:

_____

_____

_____

_____

_____

_____

· ·

4 Things/people I utterly trust:

_____

_____

_____

_____

_____

_____

· ·

SEPTEMBER

monday »

tuesday »

wednesday »

thursday »

friday »

saturday »

sunday »

SEPTEMBER

monday » ....

....

....

....

....

....

tuesday » ....

....

....

....

....

....

wednesday » ....

....

....

....

....

....

thursday » ....

....

....

....

....

....

friday »

saturday »

sunday »

SEPTEMBER

monday »

tuesday »

wednesday »

thursday »

friday »

saturday »

sunday »

SEPTEMBER

monday »

tuesday »

wednesday »

thursday »

friday »

saturday »

sunday »

SEPTEMBER

monday »

tuesday »

wednesday »

thursday »

friday »

saturday »

sunday »

Some Things I Know For Sure:

1. Kate Moss is very wrong when she says, 'Nothing tastes as good as skinny feels' because . . . pasties. Rest my case.

2. Toffee and beef just don't go together, I need to surrender and give up trying.

3. It's best to own up, and own it, when you've made a mistake.

4. False praise and unchecked hyperbole are poisons.

5. Only ever say 'I love you' when it's true. It's OK if it's true a lot.

6. My love is eternal, my patience is not!

7. We are all 72.8% water.

8. We spend 10% of our life blinking . . . (What are we missing?).

9. Hurt people hurt people.

10. Death doesn't alter love.

11. It's OK to say no.

12. Books, music and art matter, they can change you.

13. Rage corrupts.

14. Our parents profoundly affect our self-worth.

15. Fred Molina is a truly great actor.

16. Women are mighty.

17. 'Everybody needs a bosom for a pillow' . . . (Cornershop).

Now, some things you know for sure:

1.

2.

3.

4.

5.

6.

7.

8.

9.

10.

OCTOBER

So, here it is. The month I turn sixty . . . that's years of actual age . . . of being alive . . .

KINTSUGI – The 500-year-old Japanese art of fixing broken pottery with gold lacquer. Known as 'golden joinery', it is meant to encourage the embracing of imperfections, and to treat breakage and repair as part of the value of an object, to celebrate its beautiful history, rather than disguising it. The process usually results in something even more beautiful.

YES!

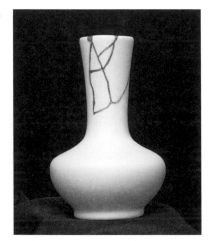

That's the spirit in which I am going to sail into my sixties. Owning all my little brokennesses, accepting my imperfections and using my hope and faith as my gold glue which will fix me together enough to take me forward. I'm going to know that each crack on me, and in me, represents something I've learnt from, and is a clue to my history, a mark I'm proud to bear.

Here I is – flawed as f**k and fine with that. Fragmented and re-purposed, here I go into my future . . .

OK. That's my aspirational grand narrative, but let's get down to the nitty gritty of the birthday month:

I have absolutely no problem with the amount of years each birthday brings. My difficulty is with the birth DAY itself, especially when it's a 'big' one with an 0 in it. That somehow indicates that we all have to go into a tailspin of chaotic stress organizing a party I don't want to go to. Yes, I AM that pooper, the person who dreads pretty much every 'party'. I have sometimes kidded myself that I enjoyed it retrospectively because I met this or that interesting person, or so-and-so said a funny thing, or the band was great or the grub was amazing or …something. The brutal truth is that, yes, there have been some memorable moments at parties, but without exception I have been longing to leave every single party I've ever been to from the second I've arrived. I can't enjoy the melée somehow – there are too many distractions, and all those annoyingly fractured conversations that rarely get beyond trivial and polite. I find myself over-smiling and agreeing with anything, in order to get through it. I am not the proper me, I'm the party me. An alien creature. An awkward, obsequious twot.

It's a bit like the instructions I remember getting when we went yomping on Dartmoor as youngsters, led by a friend's squaddie dad. We were told we had to 'walk at the pace of the slowest person', so that we stayed together. It SOUNDS like good advice, building the bond of our group. Yeah. You would hope. What actually happens, of course, is that resentment sets in with the speedier ones. They don't want to be held back, they don't really want to be considerate or merciful. They want to stride out on their own and WIN. They come to loathe the slowest person. I know. I WAS that snail. To this very day, I really dislike enforced fast walking of any sort. Almost as much as I dislike parties.

The similarity to the party scenario is that at a party it's best if you acquiesce, and interact in a lowest-common-denominator way, simply to keep the party going. People stand about in groups, keeping it going. Keep it going … don't let anyone feel left out, don't ignore anyone, have a little flurry of bon mots with each and every person, make sure you don't forget her name, his last book, their divorce, that important thing she told you last time, how he knows the host, that important thing you told her last time, don't retell a story they've already heard, don't mind when they tell you a story you've already heard, don't spit your food, keep standing up, shout over music you'd prefer to be listening to, have lengthy conversations with drunkards who won't remember a single word tomorrow and I will never get those minutes back. The most important thing is that the host should never think for a minute that the party is faltering in any way. Even though it is.

What's round and bad-tempered?

(A) A vicious circle.

(B) Me at a party.

At parties, I always seem to be trapped in a situation where it would seem rude to move away, and the person I'm talking to (usually someone I hardly know, whilst I can see my real friends, my safe harbour, out of the corner of my eye having a laugh on the other side of the room) probably feels exactly the same about me.

Now look, OF COURSE there is fun to be had at parties . . . just usually in the room I'm not in. (Note to self—maybe it's my fault?!) I love it when there's a focus like a band or a speech or something, a blessed relief from keeping the party going.

All this to say that I most definitely won't be having a party for my sixtieth, but I will be celebrating in my most favourite way, with my chap, my kids, my best friend, my brother plus family, and my gay husband. A small gathering where we all properly know each other, where anything goes and no-one will be left out, where we genuinely RELAX. I hope for good music, food, wine, stories, kissing and cake. I hope there will be some excellent swearing. I'm sure there will be some tears from me, probably about three and a half minutes after the wine. If there's all or even some of the above I will be happy.

Forgive my irascibility. I think I over-partied in my youth or something. Fact is, one of the truly wonderful things about this age is that I KNOW WHAT I LIKE. And. Time is short, so I ain't spendin' it doing stuff I don't like.

Now. Presents. Oh boy, this is a tricky one.

I've been grumpy about parties.

Now I'm going to be ungrateful about presents.

The honest truth is that my favourite present is:

NO present.

It hasn't always been like this, I LOVED receiving gifts as a kid, of course I did, especially at Christmas, when we always had one BIG present and then about four little ones. I think my daughter received upwards of thirty gifts last Christmas, including several quite big ones. When did we swell to this excess?

I find it overwhelming. I genuinely can't cope with so much incoming generosity, YET, of course I am the worst proponent when it comes to the giving part. I LOVE looking for, buying and giving presents. I have a cupboard in my house stuffed to the rafters with various gifts I've found as I go about my business. I prefer to shop like that, gradually, all through the year, rather than have a desperate splurge two minutes before a birthday or Christmas. Anyone who knows me (ask Fatty Saunders) will attest to my massively out of control gift-buying addiction. I spent most of our tours doing it in different cities. I think it is a way to keep my beloveds close to me when I'm not with them, because I am thinking about them, and what they might like. So, why do I find it so hard to accept that this may well be the case the other way round? Dunno . . .

Something to do with not wanting people to spend dosh they might not have?

Something to do with dealing with so many bloody awful hideous unwanted odd gifts from Evil Granny when I was younger? So many times I smiled and thanked her politely for the dreadful things she gave me (e.g. two small birds of indeterminate breed sitting on a log. Log was plastic. Birds were mushrooms. YES, mushrooms).

Something to do with a need to be a facilitator, not a participator?

Something to do with the obscenity of excess, and how it feels impossible to appreciate anything individual properly if there's too much?

Something to do with my dislike of clutter and tat?

Something to do with control?

Yeah. Probably the latter most of all. Interesting.

When I think back, my most favourite presents in the last forty or so years have been simple and personal. Birthday cards hand-made by my daughter. Heart-stones foraged from the beach, mounted in a frame by my husband. A tea cosy with a hilarious embroidered poem made by my son's girlfriend. A candle in my favourite scent from my other daughter.

Myself, I am RUBBISH at making stuff. I have attempted to, but I don't have the patience. I hurriedly dash at it with no skill or knowledge. The staples come out, the glue doesn't stick, the paper curls. Somehow I have the ability to make a good idea into genuinely ugly crap very efficiently.

Once, as parents of an eight-year-old, we were asked by her teacher to 'help' her make a small Elizabethan building to contribute to a living map of London. The plan was to re-create the Fire of London scenario, depicting Pudding Lane at the centre, in the school field. After several failed attempts to build a small house (how hard can it be?!), I lost my patience, then my temper, and sellotaped some paper on to a beautiful house-shaped jewellery box that Fatty Saunders had given me years before. A much-prized object of great beauty and value. We drew and painted the house on to the paper, which was to be removed when the school project was over. We proudly carried our creation into school the next day and felt a tiny bit smug as it was chosen to be placed near the baker's on Pudding Lane.

Prime location. Job well done . . . Until the Head, after explaining all about how the fire started, decided to actually start a fire, liberally dousing it all in petrol, and setting the whole ruddy mini city alight! Somehow I had completely missed that this was the point of the exercise. First history, followed swiftly by pyrotechnic chemistry – how fire affects paper/metal/wood/. . . beautiful rare jewellery boxes. I stood helplessly by as my beautiful box went up in flames. That was the price I paid for impatience, laziness and utter incompetence.

So, I can't make stuff, but I'm really good at buying it. I've always got my eyes open for an unusual little tchotchke, and I derive ENORMOUS pleasure from it, if I think I've found something just right.

As my kids grow, I realize that, like Evil Granny, I often get it quite wrong. Especially when it comes to clothes. DON'T BUY CLOTHES FOR ANYONE IN THEIR TWENTIES UNLESS YOU, TOO, ARE IN YOUR TWENTIES!!! That's my rule now.

Or, at the very least, keep the receipt.

I was utterly delighted when it became de rigueur to give people charity gifts for Christmas. Y'know – here's a picture of a chicken/cow/goat/toilet/teacher I have bought for you.

Well, not for you.

On your behalf.

For someone who needs it.

You get nothing, nada.

Except the pleasure of knowing someone else benefited.

You, personally, are giftless, ungifted, gift-light.

I thought this was a BRILLIANT idea and I spent a queen's ransom buying various curious 'presents' for the whole family.

Never have I seen such a surprised and grumpy crew as the family that Christmas Day. Everyone tried to hide their dismay, tried to be selfless, but it was clear that joy had been hijacked by charity. If I do it again, and I intend to, I think maybe I will warn folk, so that they can rehearse their 'Oh I see, yes, that is the right decision' conceding faces.

A refreshing thing happened recently when I told my eldest daughter to be honest about a waistcoat I bought her. It was a substantial item of clothing, and I didn't want her to pretend to like it if she really didn't. Well, she didn't, and she said so. In a perfectly reasonable, loving and decent way. Fine, that waistcoat can be returned easily and she can have something she likes. Everyone is happy. It's WONDERFUL to have an easy discourse about it, I love that we can.

BUT.

Would I ever bring myself to do the same? Could I look my darlings in the eye and honestly say I don't like/want/need something they've given me? I don't think so. And that's MY problem entirely. It should be possible, it should be easy, it should be open and honest, but it ain't. It's where my own rules don't apply to me. It's where I'm a supreme hypocrite. It's where I am most British and ruled by laws of ridiculous politeness. It's where I try out being gracious but end up feeling guilty.

Y'know what? THESE ARE GREAT PROBLEMS TO HAVE! Lucky me, for God's sake!

Shuttup and deal with it, Frenchie.

Another outdated-manners habit that I am helplessly chained to by dint of my mother's training is the ancient practice of writing thank yous. The joy of present-receiving as a kid was swiftly followed by the misery of the enforced homework that was thank-you-letter writing. I hated it once upon a long time ago, but eventually came to associate it with making Mum happy, and knowing it was, for us, undoubtedly the right thing to do. I seriously don't mind or judge IN ANY WAY if other folk don't, it probably means they didn't have to undergo the grim Boxing-Day or Day-After-Birthday thank-you blues. But, like any family tradition, I now value the familiarity of it. My own daughter absolutely knows she has utter free choice about whether she writes thank yous or not . . . it's also my free choice to lock her in a basement and beat her senseless with old Christmas trees if she doesn't . . . so that's that sorted then. Lovely.

One tiny little addendum I would just like to put out there. No-one EVER needs to write a thank-you letter for a thank-you letter. That way lies madness, and a never-ending spiral of hideous gratitude hell. Just . . . don't, I mean that nicely . . .

SIXTY!

Blimey, what is being sixty like?

Does this mean that perhaps, finally, I really ought to do some of the growing up I've been meaning to do?

In some departments, I am HUGELY grown up, like: organizing logistics of travel, theatre tickets, etc., scheduling events, drinking bitter adult coffee, assuming responsibility for animals, paying a mortgage, getting life insurance, updating my will, driving a proper car containing many safety features, eating Brussels sprouts willingly, knowing some first aid including the Heimlich manoeuvre, not opening presents until the day, knowing when to wear a cardi so I can 'feel the benefit', wearing reflective strips if out walking at night, not using a Brillo pad on a non-stick frying pan, NOT sticking a wet finger in husband's ear when he's not expecting it . . . stuff like that. The important stuff. I'm very grown up at that.

The other bits that might need some attending to in the maturity stakes include stuff like: overlove of Ribena, sulking, cutting my food up into little bits, the feeling of homework-not-done dread on a Sunday evening usually synonymous with the opening bars of the *Songs of Praise* theme tune, resolutely refusing to use people's titles if they have them, purposely dribbling on my brother, the desire to have glitter on my face and, if at all possible, wear strap-on wings. Crying too much. Not flossing enough. Giving everyone slightly unkind secret nicknames. Making low rumbling roaring noises when impatient. Being sarcastic too often, too loudly. Suddenly tickling people. Not eating anything with a shell or a tentacle. Having to have the last word, and putting fingers in ears and yelling if someone else attempts to. Oh, and on fingers – sticking a wet one in husband's ear when he's not expecting it.

That last one is literally perilously dangerous . . . but, childishly, I can't stop doing it, m'lud, even though I know it could end me.

I suppose that if these are my growing-up ambitions, it's entirely possible that I could achieve them. It's just not that probable, because I'm unlikely to try that hard if I'm honest. You see, one of the best things about being sixty is that I know myself and I know what's likely, and I'm not going to beat myself up about the unimportant stuff. I'm going to prioritize and scout about for stuff to do that makes me laugh, makes me cry right, keeps me on my toes, teaches me something new, or confirms something I hold dear. I'm going to seek out the quiet processes and I'm going to make my own small circles where I can enjoy all the little things thank you very much.

BECAUSE . . .

At sixty, I know that:

All the small stuff makes the big.

All the tiny minutes make one big life.

Every minute properly matters.

Live it BIG . . .

Yea.

LIVE

IT

BIG

OCTOBER

monday »

tuesday »

wednesday »

thursday »

friday »

saturday »

sunday »

OCTOBER

monday »

tuesday »

wednesday »

thursday »

friday »

saturday »

sunday »

OCTOBER

monday »

tuesday »

wednesday »

thursday »

friday »

saturday »

sunday »

OCTOBER

monday »

tuesday »

wednesday »

thursday »

friday »

saturday »

sunday »

OCTOBER

monday » ....
....
....
....
....
· ·

tuesday » ....
....
....
....
....
· ·

wednesday » ....
....
....
....
....
· ·

thursday » ....
....
....
....
....
· ·

friday »

saturday »

sunday »

The Things That Are
more Significant Than Love:

1. NOTHING.

Those Whose Approval I Seek:

In no particular order:

1. Audience

2. Husband

3. Madonna

4. Self

You?

1. _____

2. _____

3. _____

4. _____

NOVEMBER

'Whenever I feel discouraged, I remember the words of my then three-year-old after she puked carrots on the floor: "I'm gonna need more carrots"'
Jessica Valenti

What a great kid! Spot on.

Yes, that kid decided that when life gets tricky and messy, you have to refuel and head right back in, stronger and more determined.

'I'm gonna need more carrots' has become my mantra for those everyday shitastrophe moments.

I need fuel for all kinds of unexpected big life stuff actually, and I am constantly surprised by how much I seem to have in my reserve tanks. Tanks I didn't even know I had, until necessity required them. Tanks I reckon my mother had me fitted with secretly when I was young. Tanks just like hers. Tanks that magically re-fill themselves just as I believe they are about to be entirely empty. Tanks with enough for not just me, but anyone else in my family who needs some. Fuel to see us all through, eternally replenished.

Which brings me to something else a tad fabulous I feel increasingly sure about. I didn't know there was even terminology for this concept, but on reflection of course there is, because most methods that really REALLY work are already known. Humans have been sharing the good stuff for ages. Nothing is particularly new. (Except 'Shewees'. They're new. And abominable. Avoid. Unless you're on the A303 just past Stonehenge, stuck in appalling traffic and have no blummin' option, frankly. And even then, don't be an idiot and do it when you're jammed up next to a big lorry where the creepy driver can see right in and gives you a round of applause when you're finished. That would be AWFUL . . .)

Anyroadup, the idea I'm bangin' on about is called 'The Shine Theory'. Like I say, I didn't know it even WAS a theory, but what I DO know is that, as a basic concept, it really works. More than that, I think it's vital, and it's this:

When those around you, especially the younger those around you, are remarkable bright lights, don't be intimidated by them or envious of them. Bring them in, surround yourself with them, support them and celebrate them. It's like candle power: when you're all together pooling the skills, the light is stronger, steadier and irrefutable, and, know what? . . . It feels fantastic, there's so much to benefit from it for everyone. The first time I remember encouraging a couple of women to come into the fold and share their phenomenal talents was when we asked two young rapscallions called Sue Perkins and Melanie Giedroyc to write a script of their choosing (still waiting for that . . .) and failing that, to write some material for Fatty Saunders and me. We had never asked anyone to do that before, it was good to trust others, and it worked very successfully. Plus we made two new, most excellent chums. Nowt wrong with any of that, all good.

It's pointless to take someone else's success or popularity as your own failure. It's tons better to move closer to the warmth of their accomplishment, to snuggle in there where it's rewarding and friendly, rather than slink off back to your cave, tail between your legs, feeling hurt and overlooked. Women are particularly adept at both of these behaviours, I find – being inclusive and celebratory and equally being hurt and feeling rejected and resentful. I've witnessed and indeed felt both, and certainly know which I prefer.

I clearly remember when, after I backed out of a *French and Saunders* studio commitment last minute in 1991, due to the sudden arrival of our (adopted) baby daughter, which of course I wanted to keep private (nothing to hide, everything to protect), Jennifer heroically covered for me by taking the studio dates and hurriedly writing a tiny new sitcom called *Absolutely Fabulous* to fit into said dates. Of course it went on to be huge, and although she had saved my bacon, I felt a cocktail of emotions when it received such soaring praise. What was it? Jealousy? Arrogant incredulity that she could do so well without me? Feelings of rejection?

Yes, probably an element of all these, but overriding all of those ugly, difficult emotions was something much bigger and better brewing away beneath. A mixture of pride and love. Pride in and for her talent. Love for the woman I knew as my darlin' friend. Deep down, I knew that her success wasn't my failure. Absolutely not, impossible, she was helping me to be able to be at home with my longed-for new baby. I knew knew knew that, but I also wanted to acknowledge the other, unwelcome, trickier feelings. I wanted them out of me. When she won a BAFTA for the first series, I sent her a huge bunch of flowers with a card which read:

'Congratulations, you talented c**t xx'

And that was it. Job done. All feelings expressed, laughed at, forgiven and understood.

Then, and only then, when honesty was at the heart of it, could I watch and enjoy the show as a viewer, and even turn up on it every now and then.

The lessons for me were twofold:

1) Don't allow a miasma of taking-it-personally despair to infect proper love-ful relationships.

2) Find the sunny side in every tricky situation – it will DEFINITELY be there, but might involve some careful unearthing.

So, for instance, when Fatty went off to do *AbFab*, and I did *Vicar of Dibley*, far from driving some kind of career/relationship wedge between us, quite the opposite happened. We both loved the different new projects, but we couldn't wait to be back together, on familiar territory to catch up with the gossip and use the fresh energy. It made us appreciate everything we had together.

I didn't anticipate that.

I would now.

Because now, with experience, I would know that somehow, it's going to turn out fine, better even, if I can just trust all the good stuff.

Good stuff ALWAYS wins. Fact.

And at the kernel of all good stuff is LOVE.

We know it.

We know it in our load-bearing bones and our pumping blood, in our every fizzing atom.

As I get older, I know it more and I have become embarrassment-free about saying so. I realize I have become that boundary-less old bird who hugs for too long, takes your face firmly in her hands and tells you how much she loves you.

Only if I do, of course.

But if I do, I REALLY do!

I don't care if it's gooey or soppy. I don't care if it's as wet as a mermaid's Tena Lady, I am going into my sixties endeavouring to find the love in everyone I meet and everything I do.

Deal with it, British!

'Be soft. Do not let the world make you hard.
Do not let the pain make you hate. Do not let the
bitterness steal your sweetness. Take pride that even
though the rest of the world may disagree, you still
believe it to be a beautiful place'
Iain S. Thomas

Being clever and powerful isn't the only route to success. Empowering other people to be clever and powerful is properly valuable too. In that way, we can be the amplification for someone else's possibly quieter, nascent voice. It works both ways, truly. Just as I think, 'Oh look at this bright new young funny girl', my next thought is 'WOW, that's a whole new way of thinking, I'm going to try that approach to see if it works for me too.' It's infectious, it's how we grow each other well. All we are attempting to do is to be better humans than we were yesterday. If we manage that, however incrementally small, by my reckoning, THAT is success. Not to measure yourself by any other person, but to measure yourself only by the yourself you were before.

Are you calmer?

More confident?

More astute?

More fragrant?

More generous?

More informed?

More healthy?

More alert?

More thoughtful?

More patient?

Are you happier, in ANY way?

If the answer to any of these questions is yes in any tiny way, then I'd be putting the blummin' bunting out and doing the loud clog dance of marvellousness to celebrate, because you tried. And it worked. You did something, and actions prove who a person really is. It's all very well just talking about it (listen up, Frenchie), that indeed shows who you want to be, but actually DOING it? That's the golden thing ...

Don't forget, it doesn't matter if you have wobbles every now and then, just remind yourself at those moments that:

'I'm gonna need more carrots ...'

NOVEMBER

monday »

tuesday »

wednesday »

thursday »

friday »

saturday »

sunday »

NOVEMBER

monday »

tuesday »

wednesday »

thursday »

friday »

saturday »

sunday »

NOVEMBER

monday »

tuesday »

wednesday »

thursday »

friday »

saturday »

sunday »

NOVEMBER

monday »

tuesday »

wednesday »

thursday »

friday »

saturday »

sunday »

NOVEMBER

monday »

tuesday »

wednesday »

thursday »

friday »

saturday »

sunday »

Remember THAT letter? The one you might have kept in the back of the book . . .

Maybe read it again and think about posting it?

DECEMBER

Right. So . . .

December.

Russet and silver and gold and white.

And red, of course.

Acres of red. Bolts of it. Velvet. Cheerful and chummy and Christmas.

All framed, for me, with a definite edge of black.

I want to tell you something now, a difficult thing to own up to. But, pardon me, the prospect of Christmas makes me feel quite sad. This isn't unique to me, I know that, but it's a forbidden gloom, a bah humbug doomy doom that dare not speak its name.

Sorry to remove YOUR name, tiny baby Jesus so new and holy in your manger (as a kid, I used to believe it was pronounced 'anger' with an 'm' on the front, like male anger . . . 'manger'. I was anxious that you were laid in all your bands of swaddle amongst all that explosive testosterone) . . . BUT, for me and many others, it is Sadmas, I'm afraid. Every year I hope it will be different, that when I catch sight of the first twinkly tree or jolly Santa, the requisite joy and excitement will kick in. I want that very much, to catch the merry, to ride it like a wave right from the first whiff of mince pie.

Holly, ivy, mistletoe, yew . . . come on, Dickensian Christmas cheer, happyslap me in the face and wake up my Yuletide joy, will ya?

The lucky thing is that I THINK I understand it a bit. I've only gone a bit Scroogey like this in the last five years. That timing correlates to the death of my darlin' mum.

So, as the year scurries to its close, and as these twelve months and I both surrender to our tiredness, the filter is off my grief. I forget how sad I am about this until my muted hurting heart reminds me around now. This is supposed to be the time of smiles and laughter, of goodwill and mirth, and somehow all the giddy celebration is an affront to my idling melancholy. I want to be left alone to wallow in my mid-winterness. As the teatime darkness of the nights draws in around me, I want to sit for a while in the shadows. I want to take time to notice that being without a mum, without any parent, even at this silly supposed to be grown-up age, can sometimes render a person inexplicably afraid and homesick.

This is the time of year that all of us secretly enjoy returning to the dynamic of our family, as it was, stuck in amber at when we were most happy. For me, that's when I was about twelve. That's when absolutely NO-ONE expected me to cook or organize or be responsible for anything at Christmas. The biggest task I had was to wrap up a *Snoopy* book for my older brother, some watery lily of the valley perfume for my lovely soft mum, and a bottle of something Old Spice-y for my beautiful big dad. That was it, save maybe a spiky spat about washing up versus drying. Otherwise my entire day was spent on a sofa opening a thrilling present, of which there were about five max, or on the floor over-cuddling a dog with tinsel around its neck, and eating walnut whips willy-nilly. I was warm and safe and full and loved, and all was well. Not a care. I completely belonged, in the bosomy heart of my family. It's no wonder is it, that the age-old Christmas story has at its core a mother and child? They belong together, to each other. December afternoons leave me longing for that, and I begin to get childishly grumpy the closer the big day approaches, as if that's going to surely be the pinnacle of the misery.

BUT. Luckily.

Each year, for the last five years, something a bit marvellous happens just in time, and it is my own little Christmas miracle.

Somewhere around the third week of December, I get a little fizz inside me. Tiny at first, and intermittent. It happens when I least expect it, in a frosty lane or on the sighting of an old paper chain around a central light in an elderly person's house, or finding a red berry in my hood. It's a hopeful Lazarus that rises up each year just when I was convinced it was dead, and y'know what it is?

It's wonder.

Proper wonder.

At how lovely it is.

Proper lovely.

The kind of wonder that reminds you that Christmas is definitely coming. It's big and cheerful and it's going to love you into submission so you might as well surrender. It's bigger than you, and by dint of its very size and power you are going to be held inside it, the way you were as a kid.

Thanks to wonder, I AM going to find some joy in it, in little surprising places. It won't be in any forced jollity, it will be instead in my mother-in-law's embrace as she arrives for lunch. It will be in my brother's knowing look across the table as he fleetingly acknowledges who we are missing. It will be in that last moment before I go to bed on Christmas Eve, making sure everyone is safely gathered in and all is set for the morning. I will have one last revel in the blinky lights of the truly wonderful huge tree before turning them off, knowing that the next time they go on, after one sleep, it will be CHRISTMAS.

Look how I am loving having my chicks here with me, in the nest. Look how blessed I am to have a Christmas with them all. Look who taught me how to love like this. My mum. Who I am just like. Who lives on in me. Who is here in the best possible way. At Christmas and always.

OK, grief, I get it. You are simply the portal. I have to pass through you, through 'Sadmas', to get to the wonder bit. And yes, here it comes . . .

HAPPY CHRISTMAS.

DECEMBER

monday »

tuesday »

wednesday »

thursday »

friday »

. . . .

saturday »

. . . .

sunday »

. . . .

DECEMBER

monday »

tuesday »

wednesday »

thursday »

friday »

saturday »

sunday »

DECEMBER

monday »

....

tuesday »

....

wednesday »

....

thursday »

....

friday »

saturday »

sunday »

DECEMBER

monday »

tuesday »

wednesday »

thursday »

friday »

saturday »

sunday »

DECEMBER

monday »

tuesday »

wednesday »

thursday »

friday »

saturday »

sunday »

My Failsafe Signature Dish

This makes my kids' friends love me. Stephen Fry once called me a 'total bitch' (in a good way) for making it.

It's this: MARS BAR FONDUE

- Chop up and melt four Mars Bars in a bain marie (posh word for bowl over boiling water).

- Chop up fruit (strawberries, grapes, banana). Plus some marshmallows if you have them.

- Put fruit and marshmallows on plate. Pour hot melted Mars Bars into small dish in middle.

- Give people a fondue fork for dipping.

- Lean back and bask in adoration.

- That's it.

PS Maybe add rum or cognac if it's adults only?
Or thin the mixture with milk/cream if necessary.

Your failsafe signature dish:

Place your fourth and final photo here.

You might take this moment to reflect on your selfies.

Has anything changed?

WINTER

Hasting is right. Where has the time gone? To the same place best pants go when they disappear from the washing machine, or where every one of the sixteen A–Zs I've owned have gone? Or where my upper body strength is . . .? Time must be holding a busy party somewhere with everything else we've lost track of. Bet it's untidy.

It's Winter already. I know because not a day passes without socks, and I don't even like socks that much. You need socks when it's blowing a warlike hoolie and yowling icy winds attempt to nip your ankles. You need sturdy waterproof boots so that you can stamp your mark into the ice in shallow puddles. You need a decent coat . . . because your mum told you so. Sometimes in hot shops you hate your mum for telling you so.

It ain't all bleak: there are cheeky red robins, and acid-yellow gorse, the Christmas lights are beginning to twinkle, and there's a roaring fire in the hearth. If you have a hearth. And if you're in *Little Dorrit*.

Winter can be skeletal and brutal in Nature, as trees do their burlesque best to shed their foliage. It can drive us indoors to hibernate in a torpor of telly, hot chocolate, cold chocolate and chocolate, with occasional chocolate as a treat. We look for our comforts in the cosy warm. We turn our evening lights on in the afternoon and we brrr out of our windows as children crunch home from school in the sleety dark. All the colourful flighty things of summer are gone. No flowers, no butterflies, no girls in bright strappy dresses.

BUT.

Everything has its season, its moment, and it's our duty to look for the beauty. For instance, because the trees are bare,

> 'We are able to learn something more precise about
> their trunks, branches and buds. Every kind of tree
> has its own form of trunk, with a special pattern
> into which its expanding bark splits in order to
> allow growth of the woody tissue it protects.
> Each kind has its own manner of branching . . .'
> Edward Step. Nature Rambles (1930)

The same is also true for the Winter of our lives. I am considering that to be from the age of seventy-five 'til . . . whenever. We may indeed have failing eyesight and achy joints and 'shrunk shanks' (Shakespeare). We may comprise of wrinkle and droop, our once abundant foliage is a bit sparse, but our essential timber is still evident. It's the joist that props us. Take a close look at the intricate patterns of our ageing body wood.

The knots.

The pith.

The mottled bark.

It all tells our story, and it's our evidence of the type of life we have lived and are still living.

Still living.

Alive.

And strong in lots of surprising ways.

Yes, our body ages, there's no escaping that, but surely these later years can, with luck and good health, be an opportunity for lots of joyful and fruitful moments? I'm blummin' hoping so, because that's my plan. Yes, I actually have a plan (hear God laughing in background).

Here are just some of the things I want to do and be in my seventies and eighties, and beyond:

First of all, I'm grateful to be assured enough to dare to look forward like this, to embrace the chance to get older. To get wonderfully, frighteningly old. I think it's because both of my grannies lived to grand old ages, and I firmly believe my mum would have, if only she hadn't started puffing on fags at age eleven, and been felled at seventy-seven years old by smoke. I don't smoke, thankfully, so maybe, just maybe, I might pass my mum's age on the inside track? That's top on my plan.

I want to be a person who genuinely enjoys the company and accomplishments of younger generations. It's the opportunity to experience beauty and truth in a pure way. I already know that.

I want to be a safe harbour for my beloveds, in the same way my mum was for both me and my daughter. I want to put the time into forging those links properly, and making sure those around me feel able to demand my time when they need or want it. I want to be there, to be influential in the right way.

I want to notice when that might be, so I want to be less busy or distracted in order for that to happen.

I want to actively put down any heavy historical baggage, to 'bury all quarrels and contentions' (Isaac Pennington) and let myself off the hook a bit more for any harm I might have thoughtlessly done, or even thoughtlessly thought, along the way thus far. That way, any big sadnesses that could hinder me as I get older will hopefully pass on through more easily. Trot on.

I want to . . . hold on . . . it's difficult this one . . . GIVE STUFF AWAY. Form a queue! Yep, I want to shed extraneous material things, minimalize, clear out, simplify. I'm not quite ready to do it just yet, but . . . soon. Clothes, books, art, furniture, you name it. I know that once I start, I will not waver, I will plough on resolutely until I feel the unloading is done, and done right. I savour the thought of it, I look forward to it, I need it. Need to pass it all on.

I want to drop the ego if I can. Y'know what I mean – the noisy, calculating, demanding inner voice, in favour of some quieter inner wisdom I hope I will have accrued by these years. I want clarity and patience and the confidence to use both for some kind of better.

I want to use any spare time to be creative somehow, to learn something new for no other reason than joy and curiosity. Don't know what it will be . . . paint my feet? Weave a tent? Learn to speak Dutch, but with an Italian accent? Draw cats? Dunno. But something.

I want to look through boxes and photos and REMEMBER stuff with no time constraints, daydreaming to my heart's content. See if old things can have new meaning . . . see what I've forgotten.

I want to get everything said.

I want to put a stop to overthinking.

I want to have small, easily achievable comforts like: crisp sheets – clean floors – endless chocolate limes – a good dog – fresh-cut flowers – too much coffee – big knickers – Netflix – babies – view of sea – cake – best friend on tap – access to plenty of class A drugs – stories – outside brazier – bike with engine – comfy boots.

I want a lovely full body (not front) massage once a month. Someone to knead me the way only masseurs CAN. Firm and thorough. I once gave my mum a year of monthly massages for Christmas. She wept after each one, explaining that no-one had touched her body for twenty-five years or more since my dad died. Imagine that, the sensory deprivation of it? NO NO NO.

I want to feel...a kind of peace, and of course, I plan to not be poorly or cold or hungry or lonely. No to those.

That's all, I thankyew.

Now then, I suspect that the most urgent matter about this part of our lives will be that elusive, greedy ol' bugger, TIME...

```
'Time, when it is left to itself and no definite demands
    are made on it, cannot be trusted to move at any
recognized pace. Usually it loiters, but just when one
  has come to count upon its slowness, it may suddenly
          break into a wild irrational gallop'
                  Edith Wharton
```

Much as I want to avoid this speeding-up of time, I absolutely know it's going to happen because ALL of my older chums tell me so. Can I be forewarned? Can I do anything to change how I interact with time? Thus far, it has pretty much been my enemy. How ridiculous, I've made a foe of something I have absolutely no control over...

Or do I?

Presently, I feel like I drown in lack of time. It has its clutches around my feet, pulling me down. I long for more of it, like all of us. I am aware that I may only have a limited amount of lucid time left for all I know. I am currently living in that sliver of time between the madness of my menopause, now thankfully over, and the impending madness of my dementia … which I'm absolutely sure has already started.

… of my dementia, which I'm absolutely sure has already started …

See what I mean?

I am a time-starved husk of a woman. I seem to constantly live my life six months in arrears. How will I ever catch up?

I know exactly what I need. Do you know what a fermata is? It occurs in music. It's a pause of unspecified length. Everything just . . . stops. That's what I need. I need everything to stop, then I can catch up. How great would it be if I could flick a switch – everything and everyone stops utterly still – except me who goes merrily about my business doing all the stuff I'm so hopelessly behind with. I would read 422 books, write my Chancellor's speech for graduation day at Falmouth Uni, watch twelve must-see box-sets of dragon/incest/unicorn/president/meth-lab-related film, do thinking (both important and daydreaming), sleep for ages, kiss the dog a lot (occasionally on lips . . . I know. I know), all this really crucial stuff. I'll do that. Really catch up. Then, when I'm good'n'ready, I'll flick the switch again, and I'll instantly be back in the slipstream of ordinary time along with everyone else who will've started up again. That's me, cock o' the hoop, time-wise. Totally in synch with m'life.

Oh, and by the way, whilst I have you all frozen in the fermata, don't think I won't be up to all sorts of nonsense. I'm DEFINITELY having a sneaky peek down your pants, I might even nick your shoes if I like 'em, and very probably, I will lick you up the face.

Time. It's the non-negotiable currency that you can't stop counting. Have I got enough? Can I get some more? Where from? Surely there are people who have some spare minutes I could haggle for? What about horrid violent abusive murdering bastards? Couldn't I procure some of their spare minutes that they don't … what? …

deserve maybe? Sorry if that's a tad judgemental, but listen, I would consider a fair exchange. Say ... they give me a million minutes (that's about 1 year 9 months) and in return I give them . . . I dunno . . . a hatchback? A pony? Cake for life? Seems a reasonable exchange to me. Surely The Dreadful Donald Trump isn't entitled to his full quota of life?! IS HE?! Maybe I could do a deal with him? A Faustian deal?

Tiny but telling profound peek into my fantasies there ... it's quite disturbing, but you know what I mean.

We're always chasing time. So I wonder if, as I get older, I might teach myself to have a better relationship with it?

Like, for instance, I might not WASTE it quite as much. I don't mean that I will have no rest, that is categorically NOT time-wasting, but saying yes to silly things and silly people and their silly requests to spend precious time doing more silly things is going to quickly and quietly slip off my agenda. I really must not repeat bad decisions, because it has taken such a lot of time and effort to get to this small place of understanding about how I best operate. Why would I ignore all that? Some of that understanding came at a high price, all learning does, and I'd be a fool to forget it.

I am also going to address the matter of deeper relationships as I get older, both with myself and others. THAT is an excellent use of time. THAT is where my happiness is, working out how we are all connected and doing that in the most direct way, the simplest way, and then ENJOYING the very connection. The Laws of Parsimony follow the scientific principle that things are usually connected in the simplest, most economical way. In other words, as I understand it, it's OK to be thrifty and simplistic with explanations of almost everything when it comes to humans. Boil it all down to an easy-to-understand approach if you can, and don't make too many assumptions. Don't complicate it if you don't need to.

(Listening, Dawn?!)

I don't want a bucket-list. For me, that would be just another pressure to complete. I want my time to be more formless as I age, I want to be more spontaneous, do less time-maths where I'm constantly working back from every commitment to ensure I don't let anyone down, make sure I'm on time. I don't think I will ever be someone who's happy to be late, BUT, I might be able to willingly allow time instead of begrudging it.

I want a jam-packed life.

JAM PACKED (MEANING): when you make jam, it's important to fill the jar to prevent mould. Hence – jam packed. I want to choose the jam and I want absolutely no room for mould.

I don't want a chaotic life. I want time to breathe, examine the small stuff, and recognize the connections, the allness of it all.

I want to feel small in our big universe, to be astounded by the vastness of our relatively little world, but know that I am a significant part of it, however small. We all are. We leave our imprint.

I want to use my time to purposely:

> 'Walk cheerfully over the earth ...'
> George Fox

so I am going to choose to be happy whenever I possibly can, whenever it is indeed a choice. Which is a lot, I find. More than I ever thought.

I want to graduate from middle age to older age being as honest as I can manage, swearing like a trooper (a trooper who has swallowed a Victorian dictionary) and attempting to find something of beauty in EVERYTHING.

We all give an account of ourselves in the end, we are all measured in the balances. I don't want to be found wanting.

Too much.

A BIT of wanting is OK . . .

Like ALL of us, I want to mean something. If only in my own small world.

I want to make sure that those around me also know they mean something.

Because they do – it's only the truth. I mustn't overlook that.

I want to be here. Until I'm not here.

I want to be. Until I'm not.

I want to really be.

The only way I know to do that is to plod on steadily, faithfully, and trust that in the end, it's going to be all right.

I step forward.

Left foot.

Right foot.

Breathe . . .

Slowly, slowly, I climb that big mountain.

Up, up, near the top now . . .

A quick little peek back over my shoulder is a revelation . . . the best view so far!!

Huge, panoramic, astounding.

My whole life thus far. It gets better the higher I go. Who knew?

Gorgeous.

Not quite at the peak yet . . . turn back round, face the mountain . . .

Keep climbing . . .

Oh, and one tiny thing . . .

ALWAYS ALWAYS say goodnight

before you go to bed.

Goodnight.

MICHAEL JOSEPH

UK | USA | Canada | Ireland | Australia
India | New Zealand | South Africa

Michael Joseph is part of the Penguin Random House group of companies
whose addresses can be found at global.penguinrandomhouse.com.

Penguin
Random House
UK

First published 2017
005